Girl on the Right

Memoir of a Life Upside Down

Tina Truax

Girl on the Write Publishing

LINDEN, MICHIGAN

Girl on the Write Publishing LLC
www.girlonthewrite.com

Cover design and photography by Amy Koenig
www.amykoenigdesign.wordpress.com

Printed in the United States of America

Girl on the Right: Memoir of a Life Upside Down/Tina Truax. -- 1st ed.
ISBN 978-0998537009

To those who have surpassed survival.
You are more than what's happened to you.

My mission in life is not
merely to survive
but to thrive, and to do so
with some passion,
some compassion,
some humor,
and some style.

—MAYA ANGELOU

Contents

Introduction

The book you are about to read is not the book I intended to write. A memoir about the most sensitive and revealing parts of my life was not in my plan. As a writer, inspiration often comes by way of odd mediums. In this book's case, it came from a social media poster.

Two years ago, I came across a photo of four little ballerinas standing at a ballet bar, patiently waiting for their teacher's next instruction. My eyes took in the first four girls, one by one, from left to right. There she was, the fifth girl - the girl on the right. The image of this upside down little girl, non-conforming, and the opposite of the four to her left, sparked a smile and a silent proclamation, "That's me! I'm the girl on the right!"

I saw my life, the way it has unfolded, from a new perspective. I have been living a life upside down. It was that revelation which propelled me to re-define the way I thought of myself and my place in the world.

Seeing the girl on the right being her authentic self, invoked positive feelings. I smiled, chuckled, and soaked up every detail of her body language and demeanor - the way her arms strained to hold on to the ballet bar, the bend of her knees, and how her hair hung toward the floor. The girl on the right was memorable. This was not a girl to shun, she was a girl to embrace. As a woman who's struggled to accept my girl on the right nature, I was intrigued.

I set out to write a book which explored the traits I imagined the girl on the right to possess, and how they manifested in me. It was to be a witty, sassy read, full of my sarcasm and over-the-top personality. As I wrote words, pages, and chapters, I hit a roadblock; my book in-progress fell flat. It was pure crap. I stepped away for a few weeks to reflect.

As I read my carefully chosen words, I realized how much I was not saying. Sure, I lived openly and authentically, but I did not always. The ability to love myself enough to live my truth is the result of intense focus and hard work. It required me to face every chip in my life of armor, forgive those who have harmed me, and accept myself—flaws and all—without condition. She existed inside me, but I had to give her permission to live out loud, unapologetically.

I have compiled twenty-three chapters, which provide insight into the unleashing of my true self – The Girl on the Right. I present to you, beloved readers, my journey to freedom.

Part I

Where It Started

"You either walk inside your story and own it, or you stand
outside your story and hustle your unworthiness."
-BRENE BROWN

Digging to China

I gave my first blowjob when I was four-years-old. While that statement is difficult to read, it is my truth. Childhood sexual abuse left its mark on my life. I reject that I am a victim, and celebrate that I have survived, but even in the surviving, there are landmines.

It was a warm, sunny day, perfect for playing in the neighborhood sandbox. I was determined to dig to China, as all kids attempted to do in the playground sandboxes of 1979. Despite my best efforts, I hadn't yet reached my destination.

It was quiet outside, and I had the sandbox all to myself. I was happy in my solitude, until he interrupted me. I recognized him instantly. He was hard to overlook with his flaming red hair. He was much older than me, and had an air of authority about him. Most importantly, though, he was kind. His usual band of misfits were nowhere in sight. It was just the two of us.

"Hi there," he greeted, as he squatted down and looked me in the eye.

"Hi!" I replied.

"Do you like bubble gum?"

"I love bubble gum! Grape is my favorite!"

He was quiet for a moment, contemplating, then asked if I would like my very own pack of grape flavored bubble gum. I jumped at the chance, not yet understanding why he would make the offer. At four-years-old, I did not think deeper than the promise. He asked if I would like to see where he lived. I did not hesitate. He was my sister and brother's friend, familiar, and I trusted him.

His apartment wasn't far from the playground, and was close to the apartment I shared with my mom, and siblings. He lived on the ground floor directly across the parking lot from us.

He opened the door and walked in, me on his heels. The apartment was empty and dark. Once inside, the door closed behind us. He asked if I was thirsty. I shook my head yes and gave him a dimpled smile. I followed him into the kitchen, waiting patiently as the tap water ran into a small glass. Digging to China is thirsty work.

An inquisitive child, I took it upon myself to tour the additional rooms. The apartment was small - it didn't take long. After exploring the combined living room/dining room and the only bathroom, I made my way to the nearest bedroom. He walked in, brushed past my right shoulder, and sat on the large bed facing the doorway. He patted the spot next to him. I did not feel scared or threatened, or even uncomfortable. I walked over and sat on the bed.

Without a word passing between us, he took my tiny hand and rubbed it over the front of his faded blue jeans. I felt a bulge and giggled. I had not yet learned about basic anatomy, or the differences between boys and girls; however, I knew I did not have a bulge like his "down there." I was curious. After a while, he unbuttoned his pants and drew down the zipper, providing me a glimpse of the skin and hair beneath. He took my hand and continued rubbing it over his warm, hard skin, only this time he added pressure. Even at four, the irony struck me how something so hard could also be incredibly soft. I grew more curious with every new discovery. He eased me into it.

Eventually, he pushed his jeans past his knees, and freed his ankles. I was fully clothed. He reached into the top drawer of the wooden nightstand next to the bed and pulled out a small bottle.

"Do you want to smell it?" he asked, popping the top open with his thumb and placing it under my upturned nose.

"It smells like strawberries," I said, inhaling deeply. "What is it?"

"It's called Joy Gel. It tastes good. Do you like strawberries?"

"I love strawberries!"

"I do, too." he replied, smiling warmly.

He poured the strawberry liquid into the palm of his hand, then into mine. Under his tutelage, I rubbed his hard softness with the gel. He used his much larger hands to apply it more fully.

"Do you want to taste it?" he asked.

"Sure!"

He instructed me to use my tongue, licking up and down where we applied the liquid. My small mouth quickly grew tired and I stopped licking. He placed the spear shaped tip against my rosebud lips. I sucked him in. The gel tasted good, but I soon grew overwhelmed by the plastic-like after taste.

Finally, he told me to stop and rose from the bed. He walked into the bathroom. I wiped my mouth and cheeks with my forearm, watching as he urinated into the toilet. When he returned to the bedroom, he told me it was time to leave.

I left his apartment through the dining room's sliding door at the back of the apartment, as he instructed, and ventured back to the playground. I resumed my attempt to dig to China. It all seemed so normal, like a non-event, really.

I never told anyone about our time together - what he did, or what I did. I did not feel guilty or dirty, or like I was a bad girl. I was simply too young. Surprisingly, he never threatened me or told me not to tell. Despite the price I paid, my innocence as currency, I never received the bubble gum he promised.

Nine years later, after my thirteenth birthday, my older sister brought her new boyfriend home to meet our family. There he was, my flaming-haired abuser, standing in our living room, shaking my mother's hand. Did he know the little girl he violated was his new girlfriend's baby sister?

I pretended I was meeting him for the first time. He did not look me in the eyes as we were introduced, even though I looked boldly into his. I was aware that what he'd done to me at four was wrong. Still, I did not tell. Luckily, he was just another in a sea of my sister's short-lived romances. My life went on despite the interruption.

Vicious Cycle

I was nine-years-old when an elementary school friend molested me. It was this same time that I also became an abuser. Childhood sexual abuse sparks curiosity at much too young of an age. We were victims who victimized.

We rode bikes, built snow forts, and walked to school together. She was one of my best friends. We fancied ourselves streetwise and mature for our age. Living with our single mothers and siblings, our concerns over food, money, and safety were at the core of our bond. The nature of our friendship changed from its innocent origin, however, during our fourth-grade year. We had our first sleepover.

The evening of our first sleepover, my friend's mother announced it was bath time. My friend asked her mom if we could bathe together. Her question surprised me, but I wasn't turned off by the idea. We could wash each other's hair and play in the water, she said, and eventually convinced me it would be fun. I slowly and self-consciously removed my clothes and joined her in the bathtub. Nothing unseemly happened, just two little girls laughing and splashing as if they were playing in a swimming pool.

After our bath, we changed into our nightgowns and hunkered down in her bed. Amid our giggles and chattering, she kissed me. I didn't know what to do or say. Mistaking my silence for approval, she kissed me again, this time using her tongue.

After kissing repeatedly, we took off our nightgowns and explored each other's bodies. As she explored mine, she initiated oral sex. I did not stop her because it felt good. When it came time for me to reciprocate, I was hesitant. I did not think in terms of wrong or right, but it grossed me out to think of my mouth "down there." In the end, I did it to please her.

We never spoke of what happened in her bed. We had one additional sleepover after that night. I knew after the second time I did not want to go back. It didn't feel right.

When we were eleven, she invited me for a sleepover to "do things we used to do," as she put it. I turned her down. She never asked me again, and our friendship faded rather quickly. I am convinced she was sexually abused as I was, which made our actions seem normal and acceptable in her mind. Her actions at bedtime seemed commonplace - she knew exactly what she was doing.

She was not the only friend who initiated sexual behavior during playtime. In fifth grade, another friend did the same. I'd spent considerable time at her home during our summer breaks to enjoy her swimming pool. I would often ride my bike to her house and spend the day, bouncing off the diving board and doing underwater handstands. She had a pool house where we changed into our swimsuits.

After years of being her friend and guest, our friendship faced an unspoken test. While in the pool house, she mentioned how she and another school friend did *things* with each other. I asked her what sorts of things they did together. She looked at me as if I was too naïve to understand. Being the quintessential pleaser, I begged her to tell me. She showed me instead.

We spent 30 minutes in the pool house as she showed me the things I'd begged to know. I was surprised – no, shocked – that this friend would know to do these things. She was more than willing to draft me into her play. I wondered if they'd both experienced sexual abuse. I never found out. Our friendship disappeared after that day. She never spoke to me again. Maybe I knew too much.

I will always wonder how they came to know the things they did, and why I allowed these abuses to happen, and participate myself. It makes me sick what we all went through. I take ownership of my actions, and that I contributed to their abuse. I grieve our loss of innocence, and hope they've taken steps to heal as I have.

Toxic Cocktail

The onset of my first major depression began when I was twenty-years-old. I binged on fast food and alcohol, and looked forward to the next party. I believed I was living a carefree life, typical for a girl my age. In hindsight, I was running from reality. I used alcohol to numb the pain of heartbreak, my beloved aunt's battle with cancer, abandonment issues caused by my father, a contentious relationship with my mother, past sexual abuse, and my desire to live free of emotional pain. Collectively, they were a toxic cocktail, which manifested in a downward spiral.

Until my depression, I was a responsible girl with goals and drive. I had a network of friends, old and new, and a family to lean on. At the age of eighteen, I worked full-time and had medical insurance. I'd been in and out of college, but had faith I would eventually forge a successful path forward.

I enjoyed a rich social life of shopping with friends and going out dancing on the weekends. Alcohol use was nearly nonexistent. I found comfort in being in control of my surroundings and my behavior. My greatest vices were chocolate and sugary soda – and falling in love.

At seventeen, I fell hard for my best friend. Okay, I fell for him long before that, but he didn't notice, and I didn't tell him. We spent the first years of our friendship dating others, yet keeping each other close at hand. It was often painful to see him infatuated with other girls, but it allowed us to build a foundation of friendship, trust, and genuine like before we got involved.

We used each other as default dates often, going to movies, eating at restaurants, hanging out with friends, and enjoying each other's company. We talked about everything - from our darkest secrets to our biggest dreams. When he failed his driving test, he called me crying. When there was drama in his family, he called me to lament. I was his go-to, no matter the situation. He was my lifeline and I was his.

The summer between our junior and senior year brought a shift in our relationship – we *saw* each other. I mean, yeah, we saw each other nearly every day since we were eleven, but that summer we felt attraction beyond friendship. We spent most of the summer entrenched in an angst-filled push/pull, fighting the change in our friendship, but yearning to discover where our new feelings would take us.

On a hot August morning, as I was packing up the family car and heading to a week-long journalism program at Michigan State University, our summer of drama came to a head. I'd been told by a mutual friend, his former girlfriend, a week prior to my departure, that the boy who held my heart didn't want to ruin our special friendship, and decided not to pursue a romantic relationship with me. My heart hurt, but I respected his reasoning, as I was somewhat hesitant myself. The last thing I wanted to do was ruin a perfectly good friendship. As it turned out, he changed his mind.

I saw his car coming around the bend toward my driveway and knew we were headed for a defining moment. We couldn't go on as we had the past few years. He parked his car and got out. He stood in front of me for a moment and silently watched me work.

"We need to talk," he said, stopping me as I lugged my last bag to the car.

"About what?"

"Us."

He said it, the one word I'd longed to hear slip through his lips since our 9th grade biology class. With my heart pounding in my chest, I set my bag on the backseat of the car and closed the door. It was time to face the thing between us. I was excited, terrified, and oh, so ready.

Choosing to keep our discussion private, we made our way to his car. Once inside, he asked why I'd been standoffish to him earlier that morning on the telephone. I came clean about our mutual friend's confession. I told him I'd also learned he'd asked another girl out, and wondered why he didn't tell me about it. We told each other everything. It was out of character for him not to share with me. As my question hung in the air between us, my sister approached. Through the rolled down window, she let us know it was time to leave.

"State can wait," he replied in warning. She smirked to hear his assertion, having been witness to our angst-filled years.

We said many things during the ten minutes after my sister's interruption, and ended with a promise to explore our relationship further when I returned from my week away. It was scary and exhilarating to know he felt the same for me as I did for him.

From that day forward we were a couple - high school sweethearts consumed by one another. We sacrificed time with friends to capture every moment together. Our senior year of high school was a blur in many ways, but we were happy in our bubble of love.

Our relationship wasn't perfect, however; we were teenagers with limited life experience, especially in the art of nurturing love. We fought and made up over and over until we had our last fight, ripe with words and actions we couldn't take back.

He broke up with me the day after high school graduation, saying we needed time apart, but would find our way back to each other when we were ready to forge a life and family. He swore I was the only girl he would ever love. My heart shattered. I knew I'd not only lost the boy I loved, but I'd lost something even greater - my best friend. We sacrificed everything and were left with nothing.

Our last date was at a family wedding just three weeks after our breakup. We slow danced to Whitney Houston's "I Will Always Love You." I held him tight as tears poured down my cheeks. Deep down, I knew it was the end, and the pain was beyond excruciating.

I spent the subsequent months, nearly a year, holding out hope that he'd call and say he'd made a big mistake and ask me to take him back. He didn't. What he did do was come to me when he was confused, lonely, and maybe even a little nostalgic. Mostly, he stopped by when he was between girlfriends. The lyrics of Bonnie Raitt's "I Can't Make You Love Me" played in my mind and on my car radio over and over until every word branded my soul. Every word of that song spoke a truth I was terrified to admit. Eventually, despite my desire to be with him, I moved on.

I met a guy at work the summer after our breakup. He was a high school senior. It was not love at first sight, as I fashioned myself much older and more mature than him. We talked often at work. He had a good sense of humor, and was always helpful and kind. He took me by surprise one day at the time clock as I was punching in.

"Hi!" I said in my usual chipper greeting.

"You don't happen to have a red dress, do you?" he asked, without preamble.

"Yes, why?"

As it turned out, he needed a prom date and asked me to go. I was not lying when I told him I owned a red dress, and it was perfect for a senior prom. I said yes, and we spent the next two weeks making plans to go as friends. I looked forward to dressing up, meeting his friends, and dancing into the night. We decided to travel to an amusement park the day after with his friends.

The prom was fun, and I saw my work friend in a new light. He was well liked by his classmates, and showed me a great time. It was nice being a teenager without the heaviness of life and adulthood, even for just one night.

In the morning, we packed up and embarked our road trip to the amusement park. We'd been awake most of the previous night as the prom party moved from the banquet hall to a hotel room. We were incredibly tired, and not exactly up to doing the park. A few short hours after we arrived, my friend and I made our way into the park's movie theater, settled into our seats, and drifted off to sleep.

Once we returned home and settled back into our routines, we continued to spend time together. It was a platonic friendship, yet we felt a little more for each other. I told him about the boy who broke my heart over a late-night campfire, and how I lived every day knowing our story wasn't over. I warned my new friend that I believed my love would come back to me someday. He listened stoically, never contradicting my liquid courage confession. My words did not impact his feelings for me, and we continued as if I'd never uttered a word. We claimed each other at some point in our newly formed friendship, and that, as they say, was it.

He was preparing to leave in the middle of summer to serve in the United States Marine Corp. He wasn't looking for a girlfriend, and I wasn't interested in a long-distance relationship; however, that is what we found. We lived each moment until his departure as if it was our last. We proclaimed our love, spent time on the lake with friends, and shared mutual sadness over our impending separation. Our timing was bad, but our love was pure. We were just kids.

Nothing prepared us for the hardship an extended separation would cause. I tried to live a normal life while he was away, focusing on work and spending time with my friends. I wrote love letters in my free time, hoping to bring him comfort from home. His letters were my light, and I cherished each one I received.

Despite spending a couple weeks together while he was home on leave, our youth and relationship inexperience worked against us. I was unhappy in our separation, and he was unhappy in the military. It seemed we were both fighting our own disillusions with thousands of miles between us. Separation proved to be an incredible gap to bridge for teenagers. He took my calls less frequently until he'd stopped taking them altogether. During our last phone conversation, he told me it had "been a great year together." That was the official breakup, I guess. I was devastated again with my heart in tatters. While nursing my second heartbreak, my first love inserted himself into the fold, drudging up old wounds devoid of honest intentions. It was too much - it was simply too much.

On the heels of my romantic upheaval, my mom's sister, my beloved aunt, was in the final stages of cancer. She fought a good fight for nearly two years, but I could see her weakening day-by-day. Despite her death sentence diagnosis, I never allowed myself to believe she would die. I don't think any of us believed she would die, or maybe it was denial. It was impossible to imagine a life without our family spitfire. She was our glue. I dreaded the inevitable unraveling of our family once she was gone.

She was heavily medicated and unresponsive during her last earthly days. It was important to our family that she be comfortable as she transitioned. We couldn't prevent her death, but we could provide her with a pain-free end.

I count myself fortunate that I said all the things people wish they'd said in the wake of losing a loved one. The day before her death, I sat beside her bed, her heavy, cool hand engulfed by mine, and thanked her for every back scratch, birthday cake, and Christmas present. I told her how she'd influenced me as a fierce, independent woman, and that I hoped to make her proud one day. I praised her for her ability to love me, my brother, and my sister as her own, and the impact her unconditional love had on each of us. She may not have birthed biological children, but we were her kids, as she often bragged to others.

As tears replaced my words, my left knee bumped the side of her hospital bed and jarred her into a semi-conscious state. She reached out her arms and made incoherent sounds. The noise and disruption caused a flurry of family members to rush into the room and take over, settling my aunt back into her medicated abyss. I felt horrible for bumping her bed.

"I'm so sorry," I cried.

She was gone the next day.

My aunt's illness and death played a large part in the contentious relationship which developed between my mother and me. While I certainly do not blame my aunt for that, I do blame the circumstance and timing. My broken heart, paired with my mother's equally broken heart, made us irritable and short with each other. We were lost in grief and unable to find common ground. We had a particularly nasty argument one night, prompting me to impulsively move out of our family home and in with a friend from work. Due to my new roommate's influence, I quickly fell into a lifestyle of alcohol abuse and endless partying.

As it turned out, my roommate and I were oil and water, but I was a pleaser and allowed her to bully me at her whim. My alcohol consumption dramatically increased as I sought to dull the emotional pain of loss. My behavior became dangerously out of character. I walked away from a good job and couldn't hold one after that. My sharp focus became a blur, and I slid downhill rather quickly. Things exploded one night as she accused me of stealing rent money. Despite my claims of innocence, she threw me out in a drunken rage. I was left only with the clothes on my back and my car keys. I never stole the money, but I was relieved to be out of her house, no matter what material things I'd lost.

After a brief stint sleeping on my dad's couch, I moved back home with my mom. I found a job, but was not a top performer, as you can imagine. My alcohol abuse continued. I routinely went to work hungover, and often spent our petty cash fund on party weekends. I told myself that it wasn't stealing because I always put the money back on payday. It was stealing, no matter what I told myself to minimize my guilt.

Between my heartache, grief, and not understanding why I was sabotaging my life so foolishly, sobriety was by far the most painful state of my waking hours. I wanted no part of it, and made every effort to stay numb. I did not look in the mirror often because I hated who I'd become. I cried on bar stools at 2 a.m., and stumbled into hotels when I chose not to drink and drive.

When alcohol no longer provided my desired state of numbness, I added Vicodin to achieve the reprieve I needed. After a slight overdose (nothing that sent me to the hospital, but made me horribly sick), I had a foreboding feeling something tragic would happen to break me from my drunken stupor. Unfortunately, I was right.

Kind of Knew Him

It never occurred to me that I would be raped. I had always branded myself as wise to the ways of others, being untrusting and skeptical in nature. Life taught me early on not everyone had my best interests at heart. I thought a rapist would be obvious, not a creative type who wrote poetry and music, and who played the drums with passion and vigor. My rapist was unassuming, laid back, and well-liked.

The evening we were introduced, he asked me out on a date and I accepted. While he wasn't exactly the type of guy I usually went for, I chose to look past his long hair, facial scruff, and the fact that he was a musician with no day job. He gained credibility through his association with a family friend. My guard was down.

He took me out to dinner, where we found we didn't have much in common. Our lifestyles were vastly different. Despite my struggles with alcohol, I was trying desperately to make peace with life's challenges, and was attending therapy regularly to develop healthy coping skills and end my cycle of self-sabotage. He, on the other hand, sat around his house all day smoking pot and banging on Tupperware bowls while composing music in his head. His only income came from playing weekend gigs. He was perfectly content with his lifestyle.

Conversation was awkward during dinner, until he mentioned being a published poet. As a writer, this information piqued my interest. He invited me to his place for cappuccino and a poetry show-and-tell. We had a nice conversation, then I went home. We made no plans for a second date.

A few weeks later, in the spirit of friendship, he invited me to watch his band play at a Friday night gig. I loved live music and was eager to go. I extended an invitation to several friends, but found no takers. It didn't bother me to go alone.

The bar was smoky and smelled of stale cigarettes and fermented beer. I found a weathered black stool at the bar and claimed it as my own. I ordered a tall glass of beer, and allowed the melancholic rhythm and pining lyrics of a familiar song to carry me away.

The air was electric and sparked with energy. That's when his drum solo began. I listened as women around me admired his talent, saying how sexy he was with his muscled forearms and beautiful waist-length hair. While his talent was obvious, as any fool could see, his physical appearance did nothing for me; I did not see what they saw.

With his drum solo complete and deafening applause at an end, the band's lead singer announced their break. They had one set to play before closing time. My friend asked me to come outside so he could cool down. I wasn't much into drinking, surprisingly, and needed a distraction. For the first time in over a year, I was comfortable in my sobriety. As we enjoyed the crisp November air, a van pulled into the empty parking space close to where we stood. Three men emerged from the battered vehicle.

They were his friends. He did not introduce me, but they each looked me over in that sickening way certain men do. I didn't like it. I always noticed details like that. I was trained to spot even the tiniest threat. The men left us to go inside after handshakes and murmured words. We stayed outside until it was time for the band to play.

I thought nothing of going back to my stool and finishing the rest of my beer. It was just a glass, unlike my usual pitcher, and was nearly half-full. I knew nothing of date rape drugs and was naive of the dangers of leaving a drink unattended.

I woke in a dark, musty basement, sprawled on a dirty mattress. I was naked except for a sheet tangled beneath me. My throbbing head felt heavy as nausea rolled through me in waves. I was confused, my body felt broken. The coppery taste of blood assaulted my tongue. I found the source as I gently licked my split lower lip. I moved my legs and winced in pain from the inside out. It hurt *down there*.

I wrapped the sheet around my pained body. I was thankful for the glow from the small window near the top of a wall. Although I didn't have enough light to inspect myself, the dark spots on the bare mattress were all the proof I needed. I was raped.

I surveyed my surroundings, hearing muffled voices from above. I walked to the basement stairs, careful of my movements, and how my body reacted. I felt as though I'd been ripped apart at my core. I choked on the panic lodged in my throat.

Reaching the top step, I knelt so my ears and eyes were nearly flush with the floor. I listened intently to the voices – male voices. They laughed in unison as one said something I couldn't make out. I stood up and opened the door to face my fate. Terrified, I looked at their faces. There sat the men from the bar, along with my friend: the well-liked, talented drummer who wrote poetry.

"Where are my clothes?" I stammered.

"You'll get them back when I'm ready to give them to you."

I stepped back and closed the door. I made my way down the stairs and over to the blood-stained mattress. I allowed guttural sobs to escape from my beaten body.

Long after the light from the small basement window disappeared, the upstairs door opened. My clothes sailed down, landing in a heap at the bottom. A voice I recognized as one of the three told me to get dressed. Still being mindful of my aching body, I slipped on my underwear and jeans, then my bra and shirt. I attempted to bend over and put my socks on, but the seam of my jeans strained tight across the tender, ripped flesh between my thighs. I fought back tears and put them in my pockets. I slipped on my shoes and waited.

Two of the three escorted me from the basement to the main floor of the house. They didn't speak. My friend was their leader, the evidence would seem, as he called the shots. The men put me in the back of their van.

There wasn't a seat in the back of the sparse, beat up van. I sat on the metal floor and bumped around as it jetted down pothole plagued roads. There was nothing to anchor me except for a seatbelt strap meant for a missing seat. I held on tight to keep from sliding. I didn't know how much time passed, where were started from, or where we were destined for.

The van came to a sudden stop and my friend got out. When the doors opened, I was yanked by my free arm, and pulled from the vehicle. I recognized the parking lot of the bar, and spied my car parked where I'd left it the night before. He tossed my purse and shoved me to the ground. Like my abusers who had gone before, he did not use verbal threats or strong-arm me not to tell. There wasn't a need to do so. I vowed never to utter a word about my experience at his cruel hands. I knew, even in that horrific moment, my claims would be scrutinized considering my recent behavior. I would be deemed as just another lush girl who blacked out and got what she wanted. In coming forward, I would be cast as the Jodie Foster character from my real-life version of *The Accused*. I didn't have the stomach for it.

After the van sped away, I sat in my car and cried. It was my personal rock bottom. Once safely at home, I sat on the floor of my shower, under a scalding stream of water, and prayed the dirtiness would wash away.

Many weeks later, I realized I had missed my period. I went to the local drugstore on my lunch hour. I bought the cheapest pregnancy test I could find on the shelf and drove back to work. I went into the employee bathroom and locked the door. I pulled down my pants, sat on the toilet, and inserted the cup into my urine stream. I set the filled cup on the sink counter. As I held the pregnancy test in my hand, fear set in. It seemed, after dipping the stick and waiting the required amount of time, two pink lines indicated the girl who'd been living on the edge, pickled in vodka, would pay the ultimate price: she was going to have her rapist's baby.

The Worst of It

Shouldn't it take more than a phone call to commit murder? This has been one of the most passionately debated topics during my lifetime. I, however, have no interest in debating the topic of abortion. What I have is a stake in healing from a decision that no woman should ever have to make. Ending a life should be a more thoughtful decision making process than what I put into it. Fear is the worst place to harvest life-altering choices.

I was raped. A pregnancy resulting from rape or incest, according to many, holds a legitimate claim to termination. In my case, I did not take time to think about it, or to justify my actions. When I discovered I was pregnant, I never considered abortion. Regardless of the circumstances, to me, a much younger and inexperienced me, abortion was never an option.

I do not remember my rape. That does not mean I wasn't traumatized, of course, just that I have no recollection of the act that caused the pregnancy. Not only that, I don't know who the rapist, or father, was. It was one of the four men, but I have no clue which one, if not all, raped me.

After confirming my pregnancy with my gynecologist, I embarked on the path less chosen. I was not ready for a child, I knew that, especially as I was barely surviving minute-to-minute. I'd been on an almost two-year bender of alcohol, depression, and irresponsibility, and had nothing to offer. Worst of all, I kept the news to myself. That left an enormous void in emotional support at the outset.

I broke my silence a few weeks into the pregnancy. While using the restroom at work, I noticed a bright red stain in my panties. It was blood. Not a lot of blood, but enough to cause alarm. I called my doctor immediately and made the trek to her office for an exam. She performed an ultrasound to establish my baby's heartbeat. It was there, a tiny flicker on the screen. I went home that day, ultrasound picture in hand, and told my mother I was pregnant. Not the circumstances, but that she was going to be a grandmother.

Telling my mother about the rape was off limits. It was easier, and safer, for her to believe my pregnancy was the result of poor judgment and irresponsible behavior. As hot tears stung my cheeks, I told her my news. She provided me with the support I desperately needed, holding me as I cried. I made sure she knew abortion was not on my mind.

We shopped for maternity clothes, and talked about the possibility of welcoming her first grandson. She already had a granddaughter and maintained high hopes my baby would be a boy. My sister was excited to be an aunt and hoped for a boy as well. My best friend presented me with books on pregnancy, and proclaimed her wish for a girl.

Even with all the excitement surrounding me, I was empty. I did not feel connected to the pregnancy, or the idea of impending motherhood. Essentially, I was still a child myself; I was hardly anybody's mother. I was depressed and lonely. I spent my days with blinders on, going through the motions of an established routine at work. I was unfocused, unproductive in all aspects of life.

One evening, during my evening commute, I was broadsided while making a left turn. My seatbelt didn't lock. I flew across the front seat, slamming the right side of my head on the passenger door. I briefly lost consciousness. When I came to, there was a man calling to me. He gently helped me out, guiding me over to the curb. I hunched over, wrapping both arms around my middle.

"My baby!" I cried, "My baby!"

I was transported to the nearest hospital and examined for injuries, including an evaluation of my pregnancy. It was still early on and there didn't seem to be concern for the life of my child. I found that odd. Worse, I lay on the gurney praying that I would no longer be pregnant.

All testing came back normal and I was released from the hospital later that evening. I was not relieved. Thinking of the accident and my gurney prayers, the time had come to change my course. The next morning, I made my choice.

I clutched the large phone book in my shaking, sweaty hands. My heart was racing, my breathing shallow. I clumsily dialed the number printed boldly on the yellow page.

"Thank you for calling the Women's Center. How may I help you?" greeted the receptionist. I closed my eyes as hot tears stung my cheeks.

"I'd like to make an appointment," I said.

"We have an opening on February fourteenth," she offered.

Valentine's Day, I thought.

I woke up early that morning, having slept little the night before. I was told to wear loose, comfortable clothing. Did I deserve to be comfortable? I put on worn-out sweat pants and an oversize flannel shirt. I chose to wear slippers with a hard rubber sole so I wouldn't have to bend over to tie my shoes afterward. I put my hair back in a ponytail. I did not put make-up on. I did not look like me.

My sister picked me up. My mother walked me out to the car. I could see the regret and devastation in her eyes. Most of all, I saw the look of a mother's love and concern, a look that said, "I will be here when it's over."

My sister got behind the wheel and started the engine. I put my seatbelt on. Now I think about safety, I thought. The drive was eerily peaceful. The same route I'd taken to work every day, only somehow it was different. I'd have to find a different route.

We pulled into the parking lot. I took a nervous breath. I was scared. I got out of the car, my legs wobbly.

"Are you alright?" my sister asked.

"I'm fine." I mumbled.

We walked into the office. I checked in at the desk, looking around at the others who were waiting. I wondered if they could tell why I was there.

The waiting room walls were dressed with dollar store artwork, encased spotted glass, and trimmed with brassy frames. The dark brown paneling matched the commercial grade carpet plagued with snags and bald spots. I sat down in the ancient vinyl chairs with duct tape covering tears and imperfections.

I looked at my feet, unable to make eye contact with anyone. I was ashamed. I picked up a magazine. I couldn't concentrate on the article, which went into detail about the best hairstyle for any face shape. I was screaming inside.

The nurse called my name. It was time. I could leave, I thought.

I followed the nurse to a room where she handed me a long, fat white pill. Valium, it said, in black letters. I took it with a tiny plastic cup of water. I felt it stick to the back of my throat. It left a bad taste in my mouth. I took off my clothes and put on a stiff, blue paper gown. I started to shake uncontrollably. I was so cold. I was so scared. I can't do this, I thought.

The nurse came to get me. I followed her down the hall. She led me into another room. Inside was a reclining table with stirrups at the end, pointing towards the ceiling. At the foot of the bed was a large human vacuum, still soiled with someone else's blood. The wall looked like an artist had taken a paintbrush and randomly splattered red paint. There were many before me.

I lay on the table and put my feet in the stirrups. The doctor came in. He introduced himself and shook my clammy hand. He gave me a shot in a horrible place. I tried to close my thighs and keep him away.

"You need to relax your muscles," he said.

I started to cry. He turned on the machine. It made an evil roar as it came to life. The doctor put the vacuum inside me. My scream pierced the air. Life was being sucked from deep within me. I lowered my hands to push the vacuum out of my body. The pain was horrific. The nurse restrained my hands and held them away from my stomach. The doctor encouraged me to be quiet.

"We don't want to scare the other patients," he prodded, frustrated with my display.

I thought I would die. Then it was over. What had I done?

My whole body shook as the impact of my actions set in. The nurse who restrained my hands was now across the room, rearranging supplies for the next procedure.

"Don't dwell on what happened here today. Think of your future."

I cried harder, not able to accept that there would be a life waiting to be lived on the other side of the door. Did I deserve a happy life?

The doctor left the room almost immediately after the killing machine stopped. I was angry with him for leaving, not looking me in the eye before he made his escape. How convenient it must be to inflict such pain on a young woman, then walk away. In that moment, I blamed him; I raged at him for my loss.

The nurse, after handing me a prescription for something that would stop the bleeding, told me to take my time getting dressed. She said she would be back to check on me in fifteen minutes. I could not stay; I had leave. I sat up slowly, uncertain how I was supposed to feel. Cramps were slicing me from the inside out. I needed to leave that place of death and torture.

As I put my feet on the ground, my head felt hazy, drugged. The Valium kicked in. Finally, I thought. The Valium waited too long. I stumbled to where my clothes were neatly folded and stacked. I hurriedly dressed, then opened the door and ran down the hall.

Making my way to the waiting room, I found my sister. She looked up at me in shock.

"Get me out of here!" I yelled.

She jumped to her feet and cradled my right arm. Weak and fragile, I allowed her to lead. Reaching the flight of stairs that separated the office from the parking lot I stopped, sank down on the top step, and grieved.

"Oh my God," I pleaded, "Oh my God."

The ride home was physically depleting. I tried my best to find a comfortable position; certain parts of my body not contacting the seat. My sister attempted to avoid bumps in the road as she drove. We did not talk; there was nothing to say. In my head, in my own voice, I heard, "Murderer!" The voice grew louder as the drive continued. Finally, we arrived home.

My mother heard the car pulling into the driveway and was out the front door in a flash. My sister, after turning off the car, came over to my side and helped me stand. My mother moved her aside and reached for her baby girl.

"Mommy," I sobbed.

***

I have grieved for exactly twenty years over my actions that Valentine's Day. No amount of therapy or words of encouragement have numbed my guilt, or taken the sting of loss away.

It was a great loss. Not only did I lose my child, but a piece of my heart. You see, in the days following my abortion, whenever I lost blood and tissue into the toilet, I saw my baby's brutalized and torn up body. I know this was not the reality, but my mind fractured. Guilt does that. Guilt is a living, breathing beast that takes you hostage at your most vulnerable state.

Once I physically healed and embarked on a life renewed, I made a pact to clean up my act and get back to who I was before the throes of depression set in. More importantly, I vowed that the taking of my child's life would not be in vain. He was worth more than that.

I fell apart mentally and emotionally after my abortion. I lost the job I was tanking, and could barely get out of bed. Attempting to reclaim my life, I answered a help wanted ad in the local newspaper. A couple was looking for a nanny to care for their three children. Working with babies appealed to me. Maybe it would fill the aching hole in my heart. I answered the ad.

Being a nanny was more rewarding than any position I'd held prior. "My Girls," as I called them, consisted of a set of fraternal twin girls, and their precocious older sister. I only cared for the babies during the day, but enjoyed all three when the opportunity presented itself. I was not a live-in nanny, but felt very much in the fold of the family for two years. During this time, I created a life of armor, secluding myself from social settings and staying clear of men. I was safe with my girls and their parents, and that was more than enough for me.

Children are incredibly healing. I often attribute my recovery to my girls. They saved me from myself in a way. Being with them was a great way to reconnect with the basics of life. I witnessed nearly all their firsts and made sure they were fed, clothed, bathed, and rested. We cuddled, sang to music videos, and danced in the living room. I read stories before naptime, and let their tiny hands turn pages at my prompting. Their laughter was infectious, and their tears squeezed my heart. I felt good to feel connected.

Once the twins were old enough, they ventured off to pre-school. My time as their caregiver ended. I knew all the ways they'd helped me during our years together, and prayed they would remember the warmth of my hug, my lips kissing their cheeks, and how thoroughly I loved them.

Thanks to social media, I've kept up with them and watch their lives unfold. I am incredibly proud of the women they've become: beautiful, intelligent, lovers of life - my girls.

PART II

Life of Armor

"Experience: that most brutal of teachers. But you learn, my God do you learn.
-C.S. LEWIS

Paved With Good Intentions

While growing up, I don't recall a time that I dreamed of finding Prince Charming and riding off into the sunset. It never occurred to me to dream of such a grandiose future. I was focused on surviving. I did not live in a home where marriage was on display, and could not possibly envision something unknown. In the same respect, I do not recall fantasizing about motherhood. Raised by a single parent, I saw the struggles of home ownership, putting food on the table, paying utility bills, maintaining a car, and all the grown-up things that contribute to everyday stress.

I loved the idea of love. I watched romantic comedies on the big screen and fell in love with the ideal courtship and grand declarations of affection. I read romance novels and appreciated the dynamic between a strong-willed lass and her stronger willed laird. These conflicting illustrations of love were exhilarating and confusing. The exhilaration came from hope, while confusion stemmed from the opposite examples surrounding me. Even though my mom was not married, she did have a significant other for nearly twenty years. I cannot remember a time when they showed affection by kissing, hugging, or holding hands, although I did hear him call her "babe" a few times. This was contrary to the movies I saw and the books I read; however, it was my example.

I met my first husband shortly before my twenty-third birthday. I was a full-time college student and worked as a nanny. I was healing from trauma, and had mostly cut myself off from the world. In some ways, we were both at a crossroads. Life was uncomfortable and scary for each of us during that time, which made us ripe for the picking.

I left work on a warm June evening in 1998 with hopes of finding a comfortable night spot to watch Hockeytown's pride and joy, The Detroit Red Wings, play for the Stanley Cup. The city vibrated with energy and excitement. I was determined to leave the sanctuary of home and cheer on my team with the rest of their eager fans. It was a big step for me, as I had spent the past year holed up in my turtle shell, too afraid and anxious to live as a young girl should. This night, I vowed, would be different. I was going to be brave.

I chose a familiar place about five miles from home, but was disappointed to find they were at capacity. This was a blow to my carefully laid plans. Instead of falling head first into defeat, I ventured to a pub closer to home. Once parked, I sat in my car until I felt ready. After a few deep breaths and a couple false starts, I opened my car door and put my feet on the asphalt. Determination is a wonderful, yet terrifying state.

The pub was dark and stale, providing a contrast to the bright June sun. Once my eyes recovered from the assault of the darkness, with my head down and shoulders slumped, I walked to the back table. I did not want to stand out or draw attention to myself. I wanted to be wallpaper.

A friendly server introduced herself. She was an acquaintance of my mom's. That fact allowed me to relax a bit and quiet my fidgeting. The game started as my order was delivered. It was good to be back in the fold of normal life.

My moment of relaxation vanished as the pub's sponsored softball team stormed through the front door with fanfare and hollers. That's when my server came over.

"We don't have enough room for all the single people to sit alone," she boldly proclaimed, as she picked up my water and salad and placed it at the table directly in front of me.

It didn't escape my notice that a man was sitting to the direct left of where she placed my food. I scowled at her.

"Don't worry, he doesn't bite."

"Maybe I do," I said with a touch of hostility.

She stood close, looking down at me in expectation. I wasn't going to win the battle. I got up and moved to the seat at my new table. I looked at my tablemate, who didn't appear much happier about his fate. At least we were on the same page.

As you would expect from two wary strangers, we were careful not to move too close to each other or speak needlessly. We both sought refuge in the hockey game playing out on the big screen before us. As bad calls ensued, and fights broke out, we found ourselves making comments out loud. Not necessarily to each other, mind you, but out loud. Things lightened between us about half way into the game. By the third period, we'd exchanged names, lamented over past break ups, and shared our life stories. When the game was over, I found his arm draped casually around the back of my chair. He was kind, respectful, and safe. I knew this as I knew my own name. I'd found a friend. I went home with my new friend that night. We slept together, but not the kind of sleeping that involved sex. He held me all night long in his arms and we peacefully slept. That was a big step for me, one that seemed out of the universe in probability when I walked into the pub that night, but it happened, and liked it. I liked his companionship and his gentle, non-threatening way.

We exchanged numbers, but didn't make plans to see each other again. We said good-bye when he walked me to my car early the next morning. It was open-ended, a see-you-if-I-see-you kind of thing. No pressure. No expectation. I went on with my life.

A few weeks later, I stopped by his apartment to say hello. As I approached, I saw his wide-open front door, Metallica blaring from the boom box inside. He walked out of the bathroom carrying a bucket and mop. He was cleaning. I chuckled to myself at his seeming lack of concern for safety, knowing he was living in what the locals considered the most suspect apartment complex in the city. We didn't have much for a crime rate, but if something happened, it always happened there. I reflected on our talk the night we met and knew he was from a one-stoplight town in rural northern Michigan. He brought his small-town ways with him.

The moment he noticed me standing in the open doorway, he froze. Looking painfully uncomfortable, he walked over to the door and stared. I was not sure who this guy was, but he was not the same jovial, easygoing guy from a few weeks ago. This guy was uptight and rude. His body language and lack of greeting made it clear I'd interrupted him, and he wasn't interested in seeing me. I did my best to close the impromptu visit and put it behind me. I made a mistake.

I resumed my life, enjoying Fourth of July activities with family and friends, when I received an unexpected call. It was him! I had written him off. I found his initiative a welcome plot twist. He invited me over to his place for the evening. Why not, I thought.

After that evening, we spent time together about once a week. It was casual, yet different. He was funny and I enjoyed spending time with him. One evening, as we were out to dinner, he informed me he only "wanted me when he wanted me" (wink, wink).

Check please! I cut our dinner short and ushered him out to my car. I couldn't believe I had to give him a ride home. I was disgusted and wondered how I could have judged his character so wrong.

I was pretty fired up and pissed off by the time we made it back to his apartment. I wanted to reach over, open the car door, and kick his ass to the curb (you can tell this memory is still fresh by my use of cuss words). Something about his silence made me pause. He looked shell-shocked. Maybe he was confused or remorseful, or both. What I discovered, after I calmed down and talked to him, was the guys at work had convinced him I was ready to move in and play house. It freaked him out. His asinine statement was his feeble attempt at self-preservation. Understanding, I forgave him, and we went back to our playful, friendly companionship.

We continued with our causal relationship through the rest of the summer and into fall. I traveled to his hometown to enjoy Michigan's fall colors and meet his parents. In turn, he spent time at my place and met my mom and sister. We were comfortable. He didn't monopolize my time, and I did not impede on his. It was the perfect balance.

Six months into our relationship, I took a pregnancy test which came back positive. I was pregnant and unmarried, and I had to tell the father our perfect balance was about to teeter on the side of imperfect.

"I took a test today and failed." I blurted out clumsily during a weeknight visit.

"Huh?" he asked, perplexed.

"It was a pregnancy test. We are having a baby."

"Well," he calmly replied, "we weren't planning this, but we are far better prepared than most people. It's not the end of the world."

We told our respective families and friends, and embarked on figuring out how to maneuver through impending parenthood. We both agreed getting married because of a baby was not a smart step to take. We also decided not to live together for the time being. I continued to live with my mom, and he carried on in his apartment. Despite my mood swings and hormone surges, we did well together and became excited over the impending arrival of our baby boy.

We were married in a small ceremony following our baby shower after our friends and church family chipped away at us. We agreed our son should grow up with two parents together in the same home, and within the bonds of marriage. Our faith and our idealism played an integral role in that decision. Our efforts to make sure our son wasn't a bastard (our inside joke) were timed perfectly, as he arrived nine days later, six weeks premature.

In less than two weeks, I was a mother and a wife, and out of my comfort zone. I wanted to run away. My doctor called it postpartum depression. She prescribed medication. My new husband and I sought marriage counseling after only a few weeks in the trenches. We were lost. Our idealism didn't allow for realism, and we each felt disillusioned and resentful. Why did he want to change me? Why did I want to change him? We were not the same two people who enjoyed friendship, laughing together, and forging a live-and-let-live couple hood.

We made sure our therapist knew divorce was not an option. We had to figure it out, plain and simple.

CHAPTER 7

Momapalooza

I was not the obvious choice for motherhood. Knowing my former self, I can say this with confidence. I was the baby of my mom's brood, having two siblings who were considerably older than I was. It seemed as they became independent teenagers, then adults, I was just getting started. While we did a lot together, and they are prevalent in many memories, I felt more like an only child. I had a selfishness and self-centeredness that did not fit the selfless world of motherhood. Many things about my free-spirited nature and personality would seem to conflict with the picture of a nurturing, gentle, cupcake-baking mom.

That did not stop me. As a nanny, I had the luxury of playing house. I did not plan to get pregnant before marriage, but that is how my motherhood journey was forged. The moment two pink lines glared at me from the viewing window, I was a mom.

My son was born six weeks premature after a serious bout of preeclampsia. I spent over two days in a state of forced labor, hooked up to Pitocin to induce contractions, while also being pumped full of Magnesium Sulfate to ward off the possibility of a stroke. I suffered through contractions, confined to my hospital bed. We were closely monitored, poked and prodded. It felt like a never-ending ordeal. After a failed attempt with Stadol, which included hallucinations, I received an epidural and sailed on to delivery.

It took only a few pushes to birth my tiny boy. The medical student who witnessed our miracle told me I was a good pusher (good to know Kegels do work!). Of course, I can't take all the credit. The human body, a woman's body, is a powerful, instinctive giver-of-life. From the pangs of labor to primal urges to push, childbirth was going to happen with or without me. Our bodies are that awesome!

I held my newborn for only a few minutes. The neonatal intensive care team took him away for testing and evaluation. They never returned him. He was placed in an incubator to help his development along. His lungs were functioning properly, thanks to steroid injections a few days prior to his birth. It was good the doctors knew my son would arrive early so they could take as many proactive measures as possible to give him the best start. While his lungs were mature and he didn't need breathing assistance, he was born without a sucking reflex and was unable to breast or bottle-feed. Overall, my preemie was in great shape. Thanks to the NICU team, he was ready to come home after only a week.

Still critical, I was unable to see my son during the first forty-eight hours of his life. They moved me out of my labor/delivery room, a make-shift ICU, and into a shared room with a new mom and her son. I watched as she fed and cuddled her baby. Family members and friends came and went, cooing and kissing her tiny bundle. I lay on my side and cried. It was torture to see another new mother with her baby beside her. After all the work it took to get him born safely, I had not seen or held my son for more than ten minutes. On day three, I was finally able to sit in a wheelchair and make the trek to see my baby.

My husband wheeled me close to the incubator. I saw my tiny, helpless boy, lanugo still covering his skin, hooked up to beeping monitors and eye-patches adhered to his face. It was a remarkable sight. I made a deal with God that day. I promised I would be a good mom to my son, would never complain about his teenage boy eating habits, or smelly feet. I promised to put away my selfish tendencies and devote myself fully to motherhood. I wanted him to be okay, to have the best chance at living a full life. Seeing a baby as vulnerable as I did my son would soften even the hardest heart, and I had a hard heart until that day.

God listened to my pleas and we took our son home. He still had minor sucking reflex and intestinal issues, but it wasn't something that required further hospitalization. The doctors assured me nature would kick in and he would develop normally. We experienced all the new parent moments, including sleep deprivation, and shifting family dynamic. The first few weeks were tough, but we forged ahead.

Because of the way our life together as mother and son began, the bonding process was interrupted. Postpartum depression took hold and I slid into a dark abyss. Besides my brain chemistry being off track, there were many things that contributed to my depression. I am thankful I had family and friends who noticed the change in me, and a doctor who saw deeper than a quick six-week check-up. With the help of medication and counseling, I came back to myself and tried my hand at being a mom.

Life with our son was amazing. He brought so much joy to our families. He was the best parts of his dad and me, in both looks and personality. He developed normally, but fought to catch up on the growth chart. He talked, crawled, and walked on schedule. I noticed he never took risks like climbing or exploring, and that he usually lined up his toys instead of playing with them. None of these things screamed at me as abnormal. My girlfriends praised my child for being "good" and not getting into everything. They said I was lucky.

At age three, I noticed little quirks about my son. He did not like his hands sticky, or touching things like crispy leaves or finger paint. He smelled foods before he put them in his mouth. He liked repetitive sounds and flicking lights on and off repeatedly. His pre-school teacher mentioned he washed his hands more than other children during their two-hour class. We all have quirks, right? I wasn't alarmed.

Our son was diagnosed with Asperger's Syndrome (also known as high-functioning autism, or autism spectrum disorder). In tandem with being on the autism spectrum, he showed signs of a non-specified mood disorder, which is common for kids with autism. I won't' get into all the specifics for the sake of this book, but I will tell you being his mom shaped me and caused me to grow in ways that I would not have otherwise. I am sure all children have this effect on their parents, but for those of us who started parenthood with a deficit, our achievement is that much sweeter.

After multiple miscarriages and false hopes, our daughter made her rather dramatic entrance into the world. Although my pregnancy was deemed high-risk due to her brother's legacy, I felt good and happy. There were a few tears in relation to food cravings, but aside from that, I was at peace.

That peace was shattered as I was admitted into the hospital the day before she was due. I had trace amounts of protein in my urine, and my obstetrician was adamant we not take any chances for another preeclampsia episode. Despite their concerns, my labor started naturally after a few hours in the hospital. Unlike my first labor, I moved around, took showers, and walked the halls. This freedom allowed me to work through the pain as I needed, and even made my labor enjoyable. You read that right! I had three of the funniest people right by my side the whole time. We laughed, cracked jokes, and genuinely enjoyed our time together. We forged a special bond in getting our baby girl safely born.

My water broke and I dilated rather quickly. Her heart rate slowed and her condition deteriorated. She was stuck. The floor of my pelvis was not large enough for a full-term baby. Since my son was so early and tiny, we didn't expect any issues. My daughter was nearly twice his size, with broad shoulders to boot. We were in trouble.

I wasn't fully aware of the complications as they unfolded, however, when the doctor jumped off his stool at my feet and yelled for every nurse on the floor to assist, it was easy to surmise something was horribly wrong. Less than a minute from his desperate plea, a horde of nurses ran into my room and proceeded to push my daughter out of my body manually. It was life or death - her life, her death.

She was born without a pulse and without respiration. I didn't know it at the time, but a dear friend who was in the room and standing next to the baby bed, has since relayed every detail of our daughter's traumatic birth. She still tears up when discussing it. As the neonatal intensive care team was about to give up, my daughter gasped for breath. It was that close. She is a miracle. Her life and death drama did not end there. Her first weeks of life were touch and go. She spent three weeks in pediatric intensive care as complications from jaundice led to sepsis.

Why do I share these birth stories? Previously, I mentioned how I was hardly a prime candidate for motherhood. These two children, with their dramatic entrances into my life, and eventful years that followed, made me a mother. I have developed patience, selflessness, and confidence. In some ways, my children have raised me to be the best version of myself.

Of all the hats I've tried on to-date, motherhood has been the most challenging and most rewarding. As all parents know, children do not come with a manual. I suppose it's good they don't. Had I known how much work, worry, heartache, and frustration comes along with motherhood, I may not have signed on. Of course, I would have missed all the good things, too.

Being a mom is a catalyst for tremendous personal growth. There is no way you can raise a child to adulthood and be the same person as when they were born. With all the missteps I've taken in life, my role as a mother has provided spectacular moments of puffing my chest and proudly declaring, "Damn, I'm good!"

Whole Lotta Jesus

As I maneuvered through a tumultuous childhood, I counted on the Sunday morning church bus. No matter what neighborhood or city we lived in, I had a church bus to catch on Sunday morning. I was happy and willing to visit God's house.

My soul was first saved in the summer of 1981 at the local Baptist church during Vacation Bible School (VBS). Church was many things to me. Mostly, it felt like a performance. I got to play dress-up in my best dresses, my long platinum hair expertly plaited and tied in satin ribbons, and, when I remembered to grab it, an old, beat up Bible completed my look. The stage was set, my armor in place. I was ready to hang out with Jesus.

My salvation took place on the first day of vacation Bible school. We'd completed craft and story time, and enjoyed a nourishing snack. In all honesty, I was partially there for the Dixie cup of apple juice, and whatever cracker or cookie it was paired with. I asked for seconds nearly every time. Okay, every time.

Feeling full in belly and spirit, we were ushered to the sanctuary for worship. We sang "Jesus Loves Me," and "My Name is Abraham," all while trying to stay in our seats and not let the ants in our pants get the best of us. After singing and passing the collection plate, we prayed. During prayer time, with my eyes tightly shut, I bent my head and clasped my little hands together. I listened as the pastor prayed for the Holy Spirit to move our feet to the altar, and move our souls to seek forgiveness. My soul decided it was ready for forgiveness. My patent leather Mary Jane's couldn't get to the front of the church fast enough. Under the guidance of a nice church lady, I asked Jesus into my heart. I did it again the next day.

By day four the patient ladies of VBS were on to me. I'm sure they compared notes about my multiple attempts at salvation. On the fifth day, one of the classroom teachers took me quietly into the hall.

"Tina," addressing me in her sugar-sweet voice, "I noticed you've come to the altar every day this week during prayer time."

I looked at her skeptically, knowing I was about to confess my fears. I did not know if I could trust her, but I chose to confide anyway.

"I have to make sure Jesus is really in my heart. I am so bad. He may not want to be in my heart."

I confessed to the concerned church lady my deepest, darkest fear: I was not good enough, not worthy enough, for the Son of God.

Fear kept me in the arms of the church, any church, for the rest of my youth and early teenage years. I was not fickle about denomination, and there were many of them. When in the company of my Grandma Mary, we spent our Sunday mornings worshiping at her beloved Catholic church. It took time for me to learn the proper responses to the Priest. I usually lip synced or put my head down so I did not stand out. I wanted to belong, and I wanted my grandma to be proud of me.

My favorite part of Sundays with grandma was not about church at all. I cherished our after-church breakfast tradition. I usually sat through mass thinking about food.

Other Sundays, after our Saturday sleepovers, I joined my best friend and her family at the Presbyterian church in town. It was different from the strictness of Catholic church, for sure. It seemed more relaxed, although still respectful to Jesus. Everyone was dressed conservatively, and we sang hymns from hardcover books stored in the backs of wooden pews. Many of my classmates attended this church. I observed the boys as sons and brothers, and the girls as daughters and sisters. It was a different perspective. I enjoyed inclusion by a family with who I loved and spent so much time.

In tenth grade, I met a new girl in school who was a year ahead of me. She moved to Michigan from Ohio, and was on the hunt for a new place of worship. Her Christian family was serious about finding the perfect home church. I was up for a new adventure, and hoped I would find my perfect fit.

We tried various Wednesday night youth groups, Sunday morning services, and Sunday school classes. We eventually landed at a Nazarene church. We faithfully attended youth group, where we made new friends from different schools and neighborhoods. It was fun and I felt comfortable. I felt so comfortable, in fact, that when we were assigned parts to play in a Bible story skit, I happily dropped down to my knees and nailed my part as a sheep. I know, not Hollywood Walk of Fame worthy, but my "baa" was very authentic. I believed I found my fit!

"I'm a Nazarene!" I silently declared.

As my early teenage years passed, I stopped attending church altogether. I'd found other interests and put religion on hold. Like all things in life, what is lost can be found. I met up with Jesus again in my early twenties.

I dated and married a small-town man who grew up in a Pentecostal church. While I did not witness snake charming and the like, I was aware of the stereotypes of this Protestant denomination. What my husband's church had was a fire and brimstone message, a trove of songs about the blood of the lamb, and a synthesizer played by the pastor's wife. Worshippers spoke in tongues and raised their hands in prayer on a typical Sunday morning. All the families knew each other, and multiple generations of individual families sat together in the old, weathered pews. It was emotionally driven, and opposite the traditional, more conservative services I'd experienced in the past. The Pentecostal service was full of energy and drama, much like a cheesy soap opera or a B-movie. As entertaining as the spectacle was, it did not fit.

A year into our marriage, we were invited to attend a church discovered by my husband's co-worker and his wife. They were a young family as well, and on the hunt for a place to forge a deeper relationship with Jesus. I was church-tired by this point, and initially resisted the invitation. In support of our family goal to raise our children within a church family, I agreed to try one more. To sweeten the deal, our friends invited the church's pastoral couple to their home for a casual dinner and conversation - a meet and greet. Imagine our elation at meeting a couple around our age, with outgoing, friendly personalities. We didn't see a downside. We liked them, what they stood for, and were happy to join their flock.

My husband and I rededicated our lives to Christ. We were baptized during a summer ceremony, and became active members of our church. We were finally part of a true church family. Our children were loved and looked after, and taught all things Jesus. I experienced many moments of gratitude to have the means to provide this kind of environment for my family. I finally silenced the voice that told me I wasn't good enough for the Son of God.

Everything was going well until things fell apart. Our young pastor found himself without a pulpit after an affair with the married church treasurer. Church members and regular attendees were tasked with sorting through grief and betrayal, and find their way to forgiveness. The subsequent pastor and church body, except for a few good friends, did not hold the same values as ours. We chose to sever our relationship with our beloved church. It was traumatic, as we spent every Sunday morning, Sunday evening, and Wednesday evening, fed from the Word of God and in fellowship with our close friends. I finally accepted organized religion wasn't for me.

I've spent many years since then fighting against my inner voice that says I need church affiliation to fit into society. Make no mistake, I have a stronger faith than ever before. While I spent decades attempting to find the right church fit, I was unable to nurture a deep spiritual relationship. I am thankful for clarity, and for the opportunity to explore different ways, more effective ways, to grow in my faith without the bondage of expectation, pressure, or fear.

Pierced Armor

It was a warm, early June morning, ripe with possibility and opportunity as all new days are. The sun was high and brilliant, nearly blinding as it shone through my bedroom window. I was snuggled in bed with my toddler daughter, who'd fractured her clavicle in a backyard mishap with her brother just two days before. She was still in pain and enjoyed the comfort of mommy cuddles. Despite the setback, as a family, we had plenty of reasons to look forward. The dawn of summer was approaching, the school year behind us. Filled with nervous excitement to begin their high school career, my niece and her best friend spent several days practicing for high school cheerleading tryouts in the backyard.

As we basked in early morning peace, the phone rang on its charging base in the living room. I ignored the shrill ring until the answering machine picked up. I heard a voice, but the volume was too low to hear the caller clearly. I sat up in bed and stretched, then walked into the living room and pushed the play button to listen to the voicemail.

My husband worked the midnight shift, which ended at 6 a.m. Sometimes he was held over if his relief was going to be late, or if they were short-staffed. Sometimes they called him back to work before he was even home. In those instances, he went back. Because it was around that time, I expected to find a similar message. I was wrong.

"This is 9-1-1 emergency calling for Tina. Your husband was in an accident and transported by ambulance to the hospital." The operator provided no details of his condition.

My blood ran cold and I couldn't breathe. Adrenaline quickly set in. I immediately dialed a friend who worked as a volunteer EMT in our town. His car arrived in my driveway within 10 minutes to chauffeur me to the hospital. We barely spoke during what felt like the longest ride of my life. He focused on the road, leaving me alone with dark and desperate thoughts. I was grieving my husband's death. In my mind, he was gone. Maybe that was my brain's way of preparing for the worst.

As trees passed by my window in a blur, my brain played out a terrifying scenario of my husband, deceased, and me left to raise our small children alone. I thought about the house, our demolished minivan, and realized I had nothing to fall back on to re-enter the workforce and provide an income. I berated myself for leaving college, choosing to get married and start a family at the expense of my education. What I did, in mere minutes, was strategize my next steps in making it alone as a widow with young children.

When we arrived at the hospital, my friend maneuvered through the chaotic emergency room and found out where my husband was, and in what condition. We both felt desperate for answers, him as a friend, and me as a spouse. Together we learned he was very much alive, but badly injured.

I was angry. I know, it sounds horrible, but it is also the truth. I was so angry with him for being alive. My brain had not made a contingent plan and I was at a loss about what to do or where to start.

My husband was less than a mile from home when he crashed into a culvert, head on, at a speed of 60 MPH. While testing provided inconclusive, the working theory is he either had a seizure behind the wheel, or fell asleep. Brain activity on one test suggested the presence of seizure activity. This is common for patients who have suffered brain injuries. I locked on to the idea he had fallen asleep, which fed my irrational anger to boiling rage.

The root of my anger had nothing to do with my husband or his accident, however, but the realization that I'd allowed myself to do something I swore I'd never do; I depended on a man for my well-being. Dependency, to me, was unsafe. It terrified my inner survivalist beyond reason. In the weeks after the accident, I mentally took inventory of all the ways in which I was dependent upon my husband. From the clothes on my back and the food in my belly, to the roof over my head and the shoes on my feet - everything was because of him.

The accident was a wake-up call. For the first time in my adult life, I took inventory of my choices, and whether I was where I wanted to be. Even in my anger, I put a plan together. It soothed my psyche and allowed a semblance of control over my fate.

I became my husband's advocate and caregiver for nearly two years. He suffered a closed head injury to his frontal lobe. He was a changed man in nearly every way. He physically looked the same, yet completely different. It is difficult to explain. He was weary of his surroundings, depressed, and anxious. He was also dealing with an anger issue of his own, which is common for head injury patients. This once gentle, kind man became belligerent and scary. There were nights when I believed he would kill me in my sleep.

One night, while settled into bed, me with my book, him with his, he abruptly yelled in accusation, "Why are you spinning things and trying to make me look crazy?" I was jarred from the words on the page before me. There was no lead to this, or to his rage. We hadn't fought or had an argument. We were not having a conversation, good or bad, at all. What was I supposed to say?

He accused me of all sorts of things, and violently jumped out of bed. I was scared, not knowing what would come next. I thought of my children sleeping in their bedrooms nearby. I wondered if I should go to them and make sure they were safe, but couldn't imagine their father bringing harm to them. He was not the man who'd been my friend, husband, and doting dad. This man was a stranger.

I heard rustling in the kitchen, followed by the opening and closing of kitchen drawers. I sat in our bed, alarmed he was choosing a knife to attack me with. The thought did not seem far-fetched at the time. He was angry.

My husband never came back to bed that night, and did not attack me with a kitchen knife. Instead, he went outside and paced up and down our road all night long. Years later, he confessed that pacing was his way of keeping me and the kids safe. It was that close.

We experienced many more incidents of belligerence and scary behavior after that night. I was nearly ready to pack up the kids and leave him. The instinct to protect my babies was on high alert. Not long after the bedroom incident, his anger internalized and turned toward depression. His outbursts lessened and eventually ceased.

During his recovery, the doctors encouraged him to sleep as much as possible and allow his brain to repair itself. It was difficult for a mom of three to go it alone, but I believed he would be back to his old self soon and was willing to suck it up. Besides sleeping, the doctor prescribed medication to help with depression and anxiety, which made things tolerable. A full neuropsychological evaluation provided us an understanding of where the damage occurred, and to what extent. We took it all in stride and made the best of things. It was a true test of our marriage vows - for better or worse.

My anger and eventual resentment became a third party in our marriage. My husband's brain injury and depression took him off work for nearly two years. He emerged a different man. His short-term memory was severely damaged, and he processed things at a slower pace. It was an incredible change from the man I'd married.

In the aftermath of my husband's accident, I faced my dark side. I wish I could take back every word and action after his accident. I was a horrible wife, but worse, I was a horrible person. I allowed my own fears and insecurities to get in the way of showing compassion and love - it haunts me still. I have apologized on numerous occasions, but no amount of apologizing satisfies my guilt. Life is full of regret, but this is by far one of my biggest. He deserved what I was not brave enough to give.

Getting Schooled

On the heels of my husband's accident, I put my survival plan into action and went back to college. Taking this step provided me a sense of empowerment over my situation, and caused me to feel more prepared in the event of another catastrophe. As it was meant to do, going back to school provided me the confidence I needed. It also fed my insecurities in a way I hadn't anticipated.

There is no greater reminder of your shortcomings than trying to fit in with hundreds of others who don't know their ass from a hole in the ground. At its best, school was a psychological nightmare. Writing was my escape from the madness around me, even during my youngest years.

Third grade reeked with discontentment. At only eight years old, I felt more like eighty-five. I was weary at times, ruled by emotion and anxiety, and often caught up in a battle of finding where I fit. I do not believe I was happy about it, either, as evidenced by an illustrated story I have kept in my treasure box for nearly thirty-three years.

I drew a purple castle with a giant yellow and pink flower in place of a crested flag. Each object, severely outlined, provided contrast to the feathery strokes within. It is the words written under the picture, however, that proved my state of mind:

"I love my flower. Do you love my flower? I don't care if you like it. I like it. I don't like you!"

I would venture to say my feelings of insecurity were front and center.

By the end of fifth grade, I had attended three elementary schools and was about to enter the dreaded halls of junior high. I had many good friends to make the transition easier, I reassured myself. As it turned out, it wasn't easy at all. Halfway through the year, I was uprooted to a new town and a new school. I'd been enrolled in five schools within six and a half short years. Life, I'd learned, required a certain amount of flexibility and agility, and I was about to put it to use.

The first day at my new junior high, while touched with anxious energy, was equally touched with promise and optimism. I found myself unexpectedly excited to make new friends and enjoy a fresh start. For an angst-ridden pre-teen, I didn't take much time to dwell on what could go wrong.

It was important, I believed, to make a good first impression. After much contemplation, I chose the perfect outfit: A long, cornflower blue button-up shirt with pale pink flowers, and cream cotton pants that ballooned at the thighs and tapered down to my ankles. This was a true 1986 outfit if there ever was one! My hair demanded the same careful attention. I made sure my spiral-permed locks were big and beautiful.

At the advice of the school's principal, my mom took me in after the morning was in full swing. I joined an already-in-progress math class at the end of the sixth-grade hall. The only empty chair was in the middle of the classroom. I took my seat after a curt introduction by my new math teacher. Lunch came right after the bell. Thankfully, a girl in my class took pity on me and asked if I would like to eat with her and her friends. Because of her kindness, my optimism grew.

The last bell rang, signaling the end of the day. I found my bus without incident. I recognized the bus driver from one of my old schools. She was a welcome sight. With everything brand new, it was nice to see a familiar face. As usual, her signature boom box resided to her left, sitting in place by the driver's side window. A local pop music station played at a low volume. It was her ploy to keep us quiet so we could hear the music. Her strategy provided peace of mind for her and ear candy for us - a win-win all around.

"Hey babe, wanna get laid?"

In the middle of the aisle stood a skinny, pasty, buck toothed boy, who obviously thought he was good with the ladies. I gave him a wither-and-die look that only a highly annoyed girl can give and sat down in the nearest empty seat.

My mom was eager to hear about my first day, but was more than unimpressed with my tale of the bus ride. Early the next morning, she called the office and asked the secretary, "What kind of show are you running here?" Never one to mince words, mom made sure it never happened again. She then had to explain the definition of "getting laid."

I settled into school with a cross section of friendships. It was comfortable, sort of. With band the only extracurricular opportunity, I tried my hand at the oboe. I gave it my best effort, but simply wasn't talented enough for band life. With me at the helm, my oboe sounded more like a duck dying a slow, painful death.

Academics were a chore during my school years. I lacked focus on anything other than writing. I knew I was smart, yet wasn't performing in a way others would notice. Labeled a chatterbox from a very young age, I kept up my gift of gab until high school graduation.

I joined the school newspaper, varsity cheerleading, participated on student council, and was elected to student leadership. Even with all that, I still felt "less than" when comparing myself to the other kids. It seemed every girl was prettier than I was. They were thinner, had better grades, better clothes, and better hair. They were better athletes, had parents with money, and never seemed to question whether they belonged.

Once I graduated from high school, I enrolled in college and set out to get a degree. Journalism was my first passion, and I whole-heartedly believed I would become a successful print journalist. When my college studies began, I saw a darker side of my chosen field and decided it wasn't for me. I'd spent all four years of high school prepping and paving the way for a life of writing deadlines and chasing a beat. I could not imagine a world without journalism. I felt safe in words. Writing was the only activity that made me feel secure and passionate.

I gave up university life and enrolled in a community college close to home. Unfortunately, I was no closer to clarity on my path forward. At eighteen, I traded in college life for a full-time career in flooring sales. It provided medical insurance and a 401(k). I was making money and living life, but was not fulfilled. I missed school. I missed being young. I was the oldest eighteen-year-old I knew.

After a few restless years, I reenrolled in community college to pursue a career in elementary education. I came back to writing and felt the excitement of deadlines, and the headiness of painting with words. Again, distraction took hold and I quit school. I traded in textbooks and deadlines for marriage and a baby. I put words aside. I took a five-year hiatus from writing, and missed that part of me.

I'm grateful for the survival plan that led me back to college. As a non-traditional student with a focused drive and determination, I fed off every lecture and assignment. Failure was not an option.

After a year back in the classroom, I felt more like myself than I had in years. I was learning, writing, growing, and collaborating. I found my niche at school and forged friendships with my professors. It was in these friendships that opportunities presented themselves. People I respected and admired championed my success. It propelled me to do my best as a student and author.

With a focus I'd never felt capable, I grabbed onto my words for dear life and never let go. I graduated with an English degree in hand, along with the English Department Graduate Award, and a few writing accolades under my belt.

What made this experience different from other false starts? I met a professor who changed my life. He saw me through my words. He provided me a haven to explore my voice and style, examine what I had to say, and whether there was value in saying anything at all. He became my mentor and dear friend. He introduced me to resources, authors, and people I may not have discovered on my own. Under his guidance, I won writing awards, a coveted graduate award, and enjoyed publication for the first time. Best of all, I was provided the opportunity to give back as a mentor to fellow students and budding writers.

Occasionally, a person walks into your life and turns it upside down. My professor did that for me. When he reads these words, he will humbly tell me, and anyone who will listen, he didn't do anything special. I'll roll my eyes, of course, because I know the remarkable impact he's had on my life. I'm living proof that he did many special things.

PART III

Falling Apart

"I am terrified by this dark thing that sleeps in me."
-SYLVIA PLATH

Pretty Face

I've always been told I have a pretty face. I never minded the compliment, either. My concept of self-worth revolved around my physical appearance for half my life. It wasn't until my time of alcohol abuse and depression that I stopped caring. What changed, you ask? I gained weight.

My weight gain was rooted in a few things outside of alcohol. Birth control injections were the first culprit, add in food cravings brought on by hormone fluctuations from the medication and I started my grand impression of an inflating balloon. Before these things took hold, I was a petite size 4. Imagine the curious gazes of my circle as I exploded up to a size 22.

My weight gain had a purpose, which nobody understood at the time, not even me. I was intent on padding myself to unattractiveness. It was a desperate feeling of wanting to fend off anyone who could harm me physically and mentally. It was the result of abuse, heartbreak, loss, rape, and abortion. I don't know that I consciously thought of gaining weight to protect myself, but it's amazing what you see in hindsight. Did I blame my perceived attractiveness for the bad things that happened? Maybe a little, but mostly, I was just plain unhappy.

The worst of my weight gain came after my children were born. With my first, I delivered at a whopping 252 lbs. That's a lot of weight on my 5'3" frame. I lost weight after his birth, but was not able to break the 200 lb. threshold. After my daughter was born, I tipped the scales at 232 lbs. I had little energy, was in constant discomfort, and battled asthma.

Excess weight affected my daily life considerably. I could not breathe when bending over to tie my shoes, so I only bought slip-ons. Sweatpants replaced uncomfortable blue jeans. Hoodies became my staple top, with men's oversize t-shirts coming in at a close second. My goal was about comfort and camouflaging my weight, never attracting attention.

My "Pretty Rebellion," as I have coined it, migrated from weight to hair. It was a loud and obvious statement when I cut my hair off and dyed it black. Black preceded red, brown, orange, and pee yellow, to name a few. At one point, I asked a stylist for a haircut cut like that of Laura Bush. I never allowed my hair to be the crowning glory it once was. I wanted nothing that made me notable. I wanted to blend into the sea of soccer moms and church ladies.

My Pretty Rebellion also provided a slap at my parents. From early on, maybe three-years-old, I remember being fussed over for my platinum hair, porcelain skin, and sea blue eyes. I was a little cherub with perfect lips and an upturned nose. The combination was a crowd pleaser and took me far.

Like many little girls, I went through a chubby phase where I was thicker around the middle until my height caught up with me. My father wrung his hands with worry that his little trophy would end up a butterball. I found this ironic as he was 5'11" and nearly 300 lbs. Even more ironic, my father, a food addict, routinely provided me with fast food and sweets as a celebration or reward for any occasion he deemed worthy. Our time together revolved around food. In his eyes, the day I graduated from a McDonald's cheeseburger to Quarter Pounder with Cheese was my biggest accomplishment. When my son was born, premature and dripping with loose skin, my dad proclaimed, "Feed him a steak!" His hypocrisy was not lost on me.

Then there's my mother, who, in my opinion, bases her self-worth on her weight and appearance, and judges others' worth on the same. I never felt blonde enough, pretty enough, or thin enough. However, one thing she always made sure to do, something I am thankful for, was tell me how smart I was. She's smart, too, and I suspect she was undervalued throughout her life, hence her focus on appearance. She made sure to tell my teachers, beginning in elementary school, that I was more than just a pretty face. In addition to telling me how smart I was, she also warned me that batting my eyelashes was not going to pay off. What I may have suffered from in judgment, I more than gained in warning. If only I had listened and not tried to prove her wrong. That is such a daughter thing to do.

My dad never told me I was smart, just pretty. After praising my beauty, he made sure to knock me down a peg. His praise never sat long enough to absorb.

"Pretty as you are, there are hundreds of girls out there much prettier." he'd tell me in a snide tone.

Aside from my looks, my father was quick to provide a verbal cut when I achieved recognition or promotion at school or work. I suspect he didn't want his children to grow past his station in life. Sorry, not sorry, dad.

It's no wonder I sought solace in food and nurtured an easy addiction. I mean, we all need food to survive, right? With every morsel on my fork and spoon, I fed my loneliness and misery, and ignored the numbers on the scale as they climbed.

It took me until well into my thirties to silence their voices and replace them with my own. Through it all, I realized, my rebellion was misplaced. I allowed their individual issues to muddy the water and become my own. I carried their baggage like war wounds with shrapnel still embedded.

CHAPTER 12

Breakdown

I was thirty-three during the onset of my second mental and emotional breakdown. I attribute many factors to the fracture of my psyche, factors that I'd put aside and tried to ignore. To my detriment, there was no way to outrun or outthink emotional and physical trauma.

I'm not certain where it started, only that I had begun to question every facet of my life. As I examined the choices I'd made, and where my path had taken me, I realized I was a galaxy away from who I'd hoped to be. Questioning whether our current lives reflect the dreams and desires we held as teenagers and young adults is the ultimate existential crisis of a thirty-something. Mine certainly did not, but instead of taking action, I cracked.

Breakdowns are irrational. I suspect that's why the early signs didn't register. I was in a wonderful period of my life. My essay, "Ending Life," my crowning glory, put my name on the lips of a magazine editor. It was my first experience as a published author. It was also the point in my writing life when I realized personal writing was my home. I'm not sure how other authors discover their perfect genre, but mine was about sharing, mentoring, exposing, and inspiring. In no other genre have I experienced quite the same satisfaction as an author.

The thing about "Ending Life" is that it describes, in graphic detail, the process of an abortion. Not just any abortion, my abortion. Although it started out as a voluntary procedure, it turned into a forced abortion, a physical and emotional trauma that haunts me to this day. The writing process of my essay caused me to relive those painful moments as if they were happening in real time. I have a sharp sensory memory and could smell, see, and feel it all over again. Every re-write was the same, and eventually broke me. I still can't read it without crying. It is a piece I am proud of despite the pain endured in its creation.

I reached a point in my life where I had to face my painful past of childhood sexual abuse. I never told a soul about my abuse, and wasn't necessarily ready to face it for what it was. I downplayed it for so long in my mind, convincing myself that it wasn't my fault, which is true, and that it didn't affect me (not true).

I spent years lying to myself in an attempt at survival. I am sure this is common. Things left unresolved always kick you in the ass before long. It seemed my time had come, and I wasn't as blasé about it this time around.

Memories of abuse affected me on a more profound scale as a mother. I looked at my son and daughter and couldn't imagine them going through what I did. What I'd ultimately survived hit too close to home. Facing this truth caused my crack to deepen and expand.

I was in a dead-end marriage. This is not to say my husband was horrible or that we had a terrible life together. I married a man with Asperger's Syndrome, and wound up as half of a lonely relationship. I often felt more like a caregiver than a spouse. We were great friends, which is why we lasted twelve years. I have a genuine affection for him even still. To have a true state of marriage requires partnership and two participants in all areas of life. We did not have that.

Our marriage evolved into two people cohabitating while leading separate lives. We didn't do things together often, or even talk a lot. We were in the end stages of our marriage's life cycle, and I was devastated. I failed at marriage and failed our children.

We had twelve eventful years together, which included two children, custody of our niece, several moves, job transfers, family drama, and a near-fatal car accident. Having a special needs child alone increased our chances for divorce - imagine adding the extras to the equation. I did the best I could for as long as I could. I have never believed marriage is disposable and never imagined divorce would be my fate. My ex-husband would say the same, I'm sure. We are better together, not together. Facing the ending of our marriage contributed to my mental demise. The crack continued to deepen.

I was a failure as a mother. That's what I believed about myself during this time. I was raising a special needs son on the autism spectrum, and a daughter that seemed to be losing her once bright light. Dispensing my son's daily medication was an ordeal for all of us. Our mornings regularly involved frustration, anxiety, tears, and too often, my raised voice. On bad mornings, he ran out of the house to get away from the pressure. My daughter, horrified by the scene that played out in front of her, succumbed to anxiety and fear. I hated sending my kids off to school after a day's rocky start. It seemed unfair that they were exposed to my frustration. It broke my heart. It was my mommy rock bottom.

As I worked to process these truths, I sank deeper into depression. I no longer found joy in writing, my words becoming somewhat erratic, especially my blog. I found my children too much to care for and my husband too much to cope with. My appetite severely decreased and I lost weight. One of the biggest changes was my fear of aging. I was surrounded by twenty-something college students nearly every day. My age was an issue because I wanted to fit in. To combat my age anxiety, I morphed myself to look like them. I wore the latest trends, choosing clothes that mimicked those of girls half-my-age. I reinvented myself as a co-ed. I was a train wreck headed for certain disaster.

I burned more than one bridge as my mental state deteriorated. I am thankful to those who loved me enough to call out my behavior. I knew I was walking a dangerous line, but was unable to stop. I was propelled by a deeper grief than I could process on my own. This sparked suicidal fantasies and caused me to believe death was the only way to eliminate the never-ending torture of my fractured soul. It was not my intention to hurt or harm anyone other than myself.

Mr. Button Up

I was in denial through much of my breakdown about my erratic behavior. In some ways, it was an identity crisis. For the first time in my life I was afraid of losing my youth. What's more, I was afraid of losing the opportunity to experience the youth I'd never had. Does that make sense? Something happened to me, as if a switch flipped, and I no longer cared about anything other than holding onto my youth. It seems so silly now, especially since I was only in my mid- thirties.

There was more weighing on me than just the fear of fleeting youth, of course. Many things had me swirling. I could not make sense of my own feelings and thoughts, much less explain them to others. I was impulsive, reactive, and resentful, and harbored an intense anger. I flip-flopped often on whether to commit suicide or simply vanish and start over. I did not care about my children, husband, friends, or family. I couldn't clear my head of these insistent thoughts.

At the peak of my breakdown, I was prompted by a family friend to seek therapy. Whatever slippery slope I was flailing on, I am thankful for a moment of clarity that allowed me to pick up the phone and make an appointment. I knew, even in my broken state, that I needed help. I had been in a similar state before and vaguely recognized similar feelings.

It was easy to obtain mental health services. I was at the therapist's office weekly with my son, who was in treatment to manage his autism. I was not new to therapy. I'd been in and out of counseling since I was six-years-old. I spent more of my life in a therapist's office than out of it.

I was assigned to a male therapist. He was a churchy type with his side-parted hair combed perfectly into place. He wore harshly pleated khakis and long sleeve button down dress shirts, usually a colorful plaid. He wore wire-rimmed glasses with yellow-tinged lenses. I wasn't sold on the guy. He didn't seem like a fit from our first meeting. I thought my craziness and background would scare the shit out of him and compromise his delicate sensibilities. But, as I was also not myself, I couldn't exactly trust my judgment. After minimal contemplation, I decided to give him a chance.

We met weekly. During the days between our appointments, I lost myself in words. Lost was not a good thing. I was literally lost in writing! I wrote the crappiest poetry full of cliché. It was equivalent to a twelve-year-old lamenting over her crush. I want to gag just thinking about it. If nothing else, my poetry was a clear indicator of my mental state. Worse yet, I gave my poems to my therapist. Poor Mr. Button Up. At least he could see my brain's fragmentation within my words. They were not age appropriate, logical, or a reflection of my actual skill.

As we went on, Mr. Button Up tried to sort through my mental mess. I can't say we worked on anything of value. He didn't bring up my schemas (classic therapist move), or ask me the fated question, "How does that make you feel?"

I don't remember much about our time together (except subjecting him to my crap poetry). Oh, I remember the day he recommended I see a psychiatrist. That was a memorable session. While he was not able to reach me, he did the best thing for me by making that referral. It tells me he was smarter than I gave him credit. I have a hunch he just wanted to be done with the thirty-four-year-old teenager, her low-cut shirts and too-tight jeans. Have you ever seen Billy Idol's "Cradle of Love" video? It was a bit like that.

CHAPTER 14

Dr. B

I wasn't afraid of seeing a psychiatrist. If there was any fear at all, it was only because I saw him as my last hope. I was counting on him to tell me why I wasn't myself and how to make it better. I was putting all my faith into Dr. B to light the long and winding path to healing.

Dr. B wasn't new to me. He'd treated my son for nearly four years. Treating autism is a family adventure, which allowed him to learn certain triggers and weaknesses about me. Despite our years working together, Dr. B was surprised to see me as a primary patient. During sessions with my son, he was quick to praise me for good parenting, was impressed with the relationship I had with my children and how I kicked down doors to get my son what he needed. While all that was true, it wasn't a comprehensive picture of who I was and what I'd hidden from everyone in my life.

Dr. B didn't know me. I was good at hiding my darkness, tucking it away so nobody could see. I was the ultimate performer. Based on his reaction during our first appointment, my act was effective.

Dr. B escorted me into his dark paneled office. I made my way to the brown leather sofa. I chose my usual spot, mostly for comfort and familiarity. I had to bare my soul completely, leaving no subject unturned. Candor and honesty was the only way he could help me.

"Tina, why are you here?" he asked, after exchanging pleasantries.

Have you ever tried to articulate an answer too complex and loaded for words? It felt like a mental Mt. Everest. I did the only thing I knew how to do in the moment - I cried. I didn't just cry, I grieved for all the years I'd buried. All the mental, emotional, and physical pain I'd endured since my sandbox innocence was stolen manifested into a rushing salty waterfall, barreling over the steepest cliff. His question unleashed a primal grief I didn't know existed.

My time with Dr. B allowed me to feel. For the first time in thirty years I allowed myself to feel every emotion I'd repressed for the sake of normalcy. It took most of my allotted session time to catch my breath. We hadn't even scratched the surface. Before we could begin with words, I had to grieve. I never knew tears weighed so much. I felt infinitely lighter. With all the wasted therapy hours and lost time behind me, I was ready.

Our next session started with my life before the sandbox, back to when my parents were married and I was born. What kind of a relationship did they have? Why did their marriage end? How old was I when they divorced? So many questions arose, but I simply didn't have answers. The questions were purposeful, however, as it brought up my perception of not being created in love.

I was only two years old when my parents divorced. During a messy divorce, and subsequent years, especially for those who have no memory of their parents being together, it is rather difficult to imagine being created from love. That, sadly, contributed to my feelings of being unlovable. I only knew the bad stuff about their marriage, and couldn't imagine how someone lovable could come from it.

We dug into the years of my father's absence, and the last time I saw him before he disappeared from my life. It was another sandbox moment.

My dad drove up, his brother in tow, while I was on my usual quest to dig to China. I hadn't seen him in a while, and am still surprised I knew who he was, but I did, and I was excited. I jumped onto my feet and ran for my daddy. He scooped me up, hugging me tight. I asked him if we could have a sleepover. He evaded my question, continuing to hold me. When he let go, he told me he would see me again soon. Soon came many years later.

My father abandoned me. There's no way to sugar coat the reality. He abandoned me, and he left my mom with no support for their child. I can't count, on all my fingers and toes, how many nights my mom held me as I sobbed into her chest, "Why did he leave me?" and "Why doesn't my daddy love me?" Sometimes I quietly grieved, other times I was insistent she tell me why. As a mother, I can't imagine how it broke her heart.

That was my introduction to anger. I was so angry with my dad. I think I still am, in some ways, but also understand he was incredibly young when he made choices resulting in life-long consequences. He was in his early twenties. Despite my ability to reason the facts, it doesn't change the fact that my little girl heart was crushed. I was doomed to a life of abandonment issues and feelings of unworthiness.

Moving our discussion past my father, I relayed my next sandbox story to Dr. B. He took in every detail. When I ended the tale of my first sexual abuse, he sat in silence. It was an awkward silence for me. I worried he was processing a harsh judgement, or finding ways to tell me it was my fault. All the complex feelings that eluded me at the time of the abuse came crashing in. Tears filled my eyes and I hurriedly wiped them away. I wanted to have my armor in place to deflect his reaction, and tears were not part of the uniform.

"I would never have known you were abused, Tina." he said in wonder. "You don't present the characteristics of someone who's been sexually abused."

"That was the first time. I'm just getting started, Doc."

My armor, which has served me well, is humor. I use humor to deflect my discomfort, only that time I couldn't. Not in the cavernous office with Dr. B just a foot away, making eye contact and watching the way I was fidgeting.

My accounting outlined instance upon instance of unwanted looks and touches inflicted on me by various men and my peers. We covered the trial of a man I testified against at six-years-old, and how he exposed himself to me and attempted to lure me into his apartment. I told him about my rape and subsequent abortion, my struggle with alcohol, a childhood friend's murder; my abandonment issues, and tenuous relationship with my father. I continued with two major episodes of depression, my husband's accident and how I responded, my son's autism, and so much more. I stripped myself bare so I could rebuild.

Dr. B listened as I purged the details of every hurt, fear and anxiety, making notes in my chart along the way. We did this during the span of a few weekly visits before we got to my current malady. The pieces fell into place. I could feel the shift.

The trigger to my behavior was easy to spot - It was two-fold. First, Dr. B diagnosed me with Post Traumatic Stress Disorder (PTSD). I was a classic case with regular panic attacks that rendered me physically incapacitated, along with irritability, severe anxiety, and a host of other symptoms. Between sexual abuse, rape, and abortion, a scorching case of PTSD was unavoidable. There was another diagnosis at hand, and it was a long overdue.

Dr. B diagnosed me with Bipolar II Disorder. He traced the onset back to my first major depression at age twenty. Because there were external stressors that coincided with my first depressive episode, I didn't receive proper diagnosis. In addition, I had years of "normal" between cycles, which is common, but also provided delay.

Most people, I imagine, would hate receiving a diagnosis such as mine. For me, however, it was a huge relief. I finally knew why I was behaving out of character. Even though I was diagnosed with an incurable mental illness, it is treatable.

I walked away from Dr. B's office with a smile on my face, a prescription in hand, and our follow up visit was scheduled. I was still in a fog, don't get me wrong, but I was on my way. I had a purpose to distract me from my madness. Believing knowledge is power, I began my journey to enlightenment. I learned all I could about my illness, and how to live as harmoniously as possible. It certainly wouldn't be easy, but it was possible. There was hope.

PART IV

Season of Change

"She had not known the weight until she felt the freedom."

-NATHANIEL HAWTHORN

Tribe

One thing I take pride in is my devotion and loyalty to friendship. Historically, I've placed friendship at the top of the pecking order, above romantic and family relationships. When my friends need me, I run. When they hurt, I hurt. Their joy is my joy. I am one with my tribe. Because of the value I put on friendship, I have reaped what I've sown. My friends, at various points in my life, have saved me.

My first friend, aside from my siblings, was my cousin. She was the first person I'd ever felt pulled to. I missed her when we were apart. We played, conspired, and possessed a genuine love for each other. Our mothers were married to brothers, so we spent a significant amount of time together as babies and toddlers. When our mothers divorced our fathers, they remained friends, allowing us to keep our close bond.

As our mothers pursued life after divorce, which included subsequent relationships, the friendship between us dulled. It wasn't our choice; it was the result of choices made by others.

Despite the changes around us, our bond never diminished. As we spent less and less time together, I felt a void, a sadness, which I could not explain. I missed her.

Our mothers had a good friend in common. She kept me apprised of my cousin's well-being and the twists and turns of her chaotic home life. Her childhood and teenage years, like mine, had taken their toll. She suffered from the actions of those who loved her in similar ways as I had. It seemed we lived parallel lives despite time and distance.

My cousin's younger sister died in an auto accident at the age of sixteen. My need to see her, to be present in her time of grief, was overwhelming. It was as if no time had passed, and I felt the bond as strong as it was when we were three.

The day of her sister's memorial, I had one mission in relation to my cousin: to hold her and tell her I loved her. It was the most important thing to me, and nothing could have kept me away. I spotted her as soon as I entered the main room of the funeral home. She was at the front near the open coffin, her baby sister lying peacefully inside. Her boyfriend was next to her, offering what little comfort he could. I carefully made my way to her side. We made eye contact and reached for each other. She sobbed, and so did I.

"I'm so sorry," I whispered. She cried harder and held me tighter. I choked out "I love you" as fiercely as I was able.

We held each other until the spell was broken. I was not the only one who sought her out to offer condolences. It was an emotional time for her and her family. I am uncertain whether she remembers the moment we shared, but I will treasure it always. I felt her heartache, bewilderment, and the horror of losing her sister. Friendship, in its purest form, provides connection to another, no selfish intention or expectation. Sometimes, it is simply being there.

That's how I learned what friendship, true friendship, requires. No matter how much time passes, no matter the distance or issues between you, true friendship carries on. The love and respect you feel for a friend never quite vanquishes - like my cousin and me. It had been years since we last saw each other, but time made no impact on my heart. She was hurting and I provided a moment of comfort.

My first friendship set me up for the friendship circle I have today. I mentioned earlier that my friends have played key roles in my life, even saved me on occasion. It started with my pre-teen years. Hormones wreak havoc with emotions and attitude in a profound way.

My thirteenth year was especially challenging. I came face-to-face with my first abuser. I spent time with him and pretended nothing was out of the ordinary. While I was not actually forced, I also wasn't of a mind to confess. My emotional energy was spent by the time he disappeared from my life. I was also dealing with daddy issues and feelings of worthlessness. Oh, and my mom was in the throes of a menopausal psychosis (that's a story for another day). The angst of puberty magnified everything.

I stumbled into the gray area of hopelessness and wondered if everyone in my life would be better off without me. I envisioned my funeral, and the notes I would write to those who'd made my life a living hell. From school bullies to family members, each note meticulously drafted in my mind. I even had a suicide plan.

***

It was a typical weekend sleepover with my best friend. We lazed around in her bedroom, chatting about the things that thirteen-year-old girls do. I loved her room, with its lime green shag carpet and geometric patterned wallpaper. It was cutting-edge cool compared to my whimsical unicorn bedroom at home. Looking back, our bedrooms were an accurate reflection of our tastes and personalities.

She had a daybed with a trundle tucked beneath. That's where I slept. I was happy to have a real bed to sleep in, instead of sleeping on a couch. It made me feel welcome and comfortable. We talked of the boys we liked, hairstyles, and clothing trends. Somehow, we ventured into my painful existence. I told her I wanted to die.

"One day," I warned her, "I'm not sure when, but I will just be gone." Whatever was in my voice, she believed me. Uncertain whether it was my sadness or sincerity, she cried. I didn't mean to make her cry, but I was careless with my confession, as well as the impact it delivered. I hate that I hurt her. We bounced back from the seriousness quickly and resumed our sleepover banter.

A week later, I was confronted by my mother. My confession terribly upset my best friend. I denied it at first, not wanting to get into a long, drawn-out conversation. I was at the age where I believed nobody understood me and nobody cared about me. I was alone, just my plotting, and me waiting to carry out my plan. My mom had none of it. She gave me the "talk to me" look, so I did.

I told my mother of my plan to end my life while walking home from the bus stop. I fantasized of stepping onto the busy road and dying instantly as a random car slammed into my petite body, slamming the life out of me. There was no pain in instant death, I'd hoped.

My mom shared my best friend's distress over the thought of losing me. She didn't divulge my secret willingly until her mother noticed she wasn't quite herself. It was her mother's concern that allowed her to unload the heaviness of her burden. I am thankful she did. Knowing I was valued, even to one person, took the urgency out of my desire to end my life.

Her initial intervention wasn't the first time she came to my rescue. As my life-long friend, she's seen me through a host of big moments, both good and bad. I can say, without hesitation, I made it through the bad moments because of her support, loyalty, and unconditional love. She loved me when I was unlovable. That's the thing with friends - they see the value we often can't see in ourselves. My friends see things in me that I am blind to.

There was never a time more important for me to lean on my tribe than in the years following my breakdown. As I flubbed my way through necessary lifestyle changes, learning how to live productively with mental illness, they stepped up, rolled up their sleeves, and jumped in the trenches with me.

One of my dear friends, who's been my rock for the past ten years, has my mood cycles nearly down to a science. She is in tune with my patterns and recognizes when the dark curtain of depression is closing in. My pattern, as we've noticed, begins with self-imposed isolation, followed by irritability and overwhelming sadness. A lack of responsiveness to texts and phone calls is when she prompts me, making me aware of what's happening. With her prompting, I work my way out of the fog with the support of my therapist and doctor. I wish everyone suffering from bipolar had a friend like her.

Since the dawn of social media, like many others, I've enjoyed the blessing of reconnecting with old friends, as well as connecting with new friends. This has allowed me to thoughtfully examine the quality of my relationships and weed out those who don't have my best interests at heart. This purging of people is painful, but necessary; It is a health issue for me. I have been careful with my environment, and those who I interact. I've created a world of positivity, empowerment, and inspiration. This is crucial to my stability. It's far too easy to sink low in the presence of negativity.

As I re-evaluated my lifestyle and made changes, my tribe surrounded me with love, encouragement, and hope. They offered perspective and helped me face the steps I needed to take to create my best life. From a career shift to divorce, and everything that came after, they were with me at every turn.

Like most people, I am most comfortable in the role of giver than receiver. I wasn't always a selfless giver, in the spirit of full disclosure, especially as a young person struggling to survive. I was in a constant fight for mental and emotional well-being, and hardly felt had anything of value to offer others. I've offered what I could, however, in the form of laughter and kind words.

My tribe has made me a humbler receiver as they surrounded me during my darkest hours. They effected my heart as they came to my rescue with their prayers, uplifting sentiments, and even financial relief. I learned to say "thank you" without disclaimers or tears. I fully received for the first time in my life.

Once I learned to fully receive, I became a selfless giver. I now seek ways to pay it forward in honor of my tribe. I remain indebted to them for this life lesson, and for making me better.

They say you get what you give, and while I will never feel like I give enough, boy have I received! I pray I am an equally supportive light to each member of my tribe. The dance we do reminds me I am rich beyond measure. Things are just things, but these people? They are everything good and right.

Doggy Paddle

Remember when you learned to swim? The doggy paddle was likely the first thing you were taught, aside from floating. It provides you that in-between place where your head is just above water, yet your arms and legs work furiously below the surface to keep you from going under. You're not quite swimming, but not quite sinking. While your body is working its hardest to keep you afloat, you make no forward or backward progress. You are stagnant. After my breakdown, the doggy paddle was a microcosm of space where I lived, yet not fully. It was certainly not sustainable.

Sometimes there are choices we come face-to-face with in life, even before we're ready. The luxury of burying my head in the sand evaporated the moment of my bipolar diagnosis. I forced myself to look at my schooling, career, marriage, parenting style, and the impact of my illness on each, and vice versa.

At a time when I felt pulled in a thousand directions, I was thankful I'd taken the first step concerning my continuing education. With one degree under my belt, I was determined to stay the course. The relationship between school and career is a no-brainer. Without a quality education, there is no career. On the other hand, as an adult, there is no schooling without the income provided by a career.

It was around this time an old friend, while going through the darkness of divorce himself, popped back into my life. He was a force, for sure! We'd known each other since age eleven and had faced nearly every stage of life together. His sadness was difficult to watch, especially as it manifested into a careless, burn-the-candle-at-both-ends lifestyle. I watched him sink deeper and deeper with the wrong crowd. He surrounded himself with takers; everybody wanted a piece of him, and felt no remorse in using his trust and friendship and partied beside him while he footed the bill.

He spent a whole summer staying with us on and off. My kids loved it. He was a great surrogate uncle, especially for a man who had no kids of his own. He was easy-going in the face of autism meltdowns, and proved his salt as a trampoline jumping buddy.

During his visits, we sat up all night reminiscing about past loves and teenage scandals over coffee. Our rekindled friendship was exactly what I needed at exactly the right time. In turn, being there for him took my mind off the exhaustion of being stagnant and lost.

As it goes with life-long friends, they know where you came from, and are quick to remind you, and are often the first ones to speak up when you fall off track. I spent months watching my friend deal with the pain of losing a marriage and life he thought would always be his. What I didn't realize was he was also watching his friend, me, caught in a life that wasn't a reflection of who I was.

On the last day of my friend's visit, he found me sitting alone on my bed, gazing blankly at the wall. I was reflecting on the fun we'd had together, reminding me of the Tina I used to be. In reconnecting with old friends, I'd also reconnected with myself. That is, the self who wasn't doing time in a self-imposed box.

"How did you get here?" he asked, as he sat on the bed beside me.

"What do you mean?" I replied, feigning innocence.

"You know what I mean. Who are you? This isn't the Tina I know. This isn't what you wanted for yourself."

I couldn't fool him.

"I know," I mumbled, looking down at my twisted fingers sitting on my lap.

"What are you going to do about it?"

I didn't respond. I couldn't respond. I didn't have the answer to his question. I knew I had to do *something*, but was unsure of my next steps. It terrified me. The idea of making any small or large changes, progressing from doggy paddle to swimming, rendered me emotionally and mentally paralyzed. That said, I couldn't afford to remain as I was. While my friend provided a voice to the question, those eight words plagued my sleeping and waking hours long before his visit.

I needed a plan and to find a reliable source of income. That was my starting point, and as far as I was capable of planning. I didn't have an end goal in mind, and didn't envision my future. I knew I wanted to feel like me again. I needed to feel my life, my daily existence, was purposeful. I wanted to learn new things. The nerd in me was itching for input. I wanted to flex my brain muscle.

In addition to my need to learn, was my need to feel valuable and valued. Some would say that raising kids is valuable, but you must admit, it is oftentimes a thankless job. Rewarding as childrearing is, I needed something outside of motherhood. I struggled with that need. I berated myself for desiring an identity outside of being my children's mother. But there it was, a real and tangible need.

In hindsight, my first step in finding a reliable source of income was a subconscious move toward other life changes. It is highly possible my brain recognized the need for life adjustments and spoon-fed information as a self-preservation tactic. This theory makes sense, as I tend to be a big picture thinker, overwhelming me at times. I was not in the best emotional place for a comprehensive life overhaul. Focusing on one change at a time worked wonders. Thank you, brain, for having my back.

Means to an End

I often had a difficult time identifying, narrowing down, and focusing on my optimal career. I didn't embark on the traditional four years of college right out of high school and begin my forever career at twenty-two. I took a Sunday drive to degree hood, and the same Sunday drive to find my perfect career. Despite the long and winding road to career fulfillment, I learned a great deal about myself and my capabilities. I sold myself short for far too long.

I went to work for a women's clothing retailer during my last year of high school. I made a modest income and discovered I had a talent for talking to strangers and uncovering their needs. It was the first time I found myself supporting girls and women with body issues and low self-esteem. I made it my mission to uplift and compliment each customer, and to be honest and helpful about their clothing choices.

My kindness filter was always in place. I was constantly asked, "Does this make me look fat?" Heavy doesn't have to equate to sloppy, and that is what I think most women were asking. Although I was a clerk in a clothing store, I felt more like a therapist.

At eighteen, I answered a newspaper ad for a receptionist position with a flooring company in my hometown. They had both residential and commercial divisions, along with providing custom flooring for trade shows across the United States. It was a good company with a niche business. Of course, I didn't know any of this when the hiring manager called me for an interview. I met with her not long after I applied. It was my first "big girl" interview. I'm thankful I didn't understand the weight of an interview at the time, which allowed me to engage in a relaxing, fun conversation. I was perfectly myself without the nervousness that would plague my later years.

I received a call from the hiring manager within a day of my interview. She offered me an administrative position, supporting executive management and traveling when needed.

"I think there's been a mistake," I explained, "I applied for a receptionist position."

She chuckled at my honesty and replied, "I know you did, but I think you will be perfect for this position."

"Am I qualified?" I politely inquired, insecurity seeping into my voice.

She assured me I would do just fine. She told me the pay rate and the additional requirements of the position. We discussed health insurance and the company's retirement plan - something called 401(k). I hung up the phone in a daze, and sought out my mom to tell her the news. Seeing my confusion, she explained my job offer was a big deal. Her excitement was contagious. I called my friends and family to tell them of my good fortune. It was a wonderful opportunity, and a chance to make my mark.

While I did well in the administrative role, it was easy for my employer to see my talent with people. Specifically, I was talented in building relationships with people who found me trustworthy, knowledgeable, and likable. My employer eventually placed me in the residential sales department. I rolled with the change rather seamlessly. I wasn't necessarily career minded, but liked my job. As retail typically goes, the hours were long and tiring.

After two years of crazy hours, I was exhausted. I quit my job without having another in place. Thankfully, I landed a new position after only a week of unemployment. From a flooring salesperson to an optician in a private medical practice, my career journey took a drastic turn...or did it? You see, people are people, no matter the backdrop. I went from selling carpet and tile, to selling eyeglass frames and lenses. While the product changed, building relationships and trust was the same.

As I moved through life and career, no job was more critical than the one I landed on the heels of my breakdown. After applying on a whim, I passed a phone screen and moved on to a half day of on-site interviews with several managers and a vice president. I walked away with certainty that I would get the job.

A representative from human resources called three weeks later and made an offer I could not refuse. It was a fantastic opportunity and paid the kind of salary I'd hoped to achieve.

CHAPTER 18

Moving On

The term "moving on" is incredibly misleading. Moving on is indicative of moving forward; however, moving forward often requires a few steps backwards. This is true for those of us who face new chapters. My new chapter was especially difficult. I ended a twelve-year marriage to someone I genuinely liked. Who does that? I did, and it was the best thing I've ever done for myself and someone else.

The thing with marriage, especially other people's marriages, is that you can't judge what you don't understand. Outsiders only know what they see, or what you and your spouse allow them to see. My ex-husband and I lived in a world of marital transparency. We struggled individually and as a couple since the early weeks of our marriage, which led us to counseling at the first signs of strife. We'd agreed, before we took our vows, divorce was not an option. We felt we owed it to each other and our family to work through whatever we faced as a team. Our dedicated approach and philosophy made the reality of our impending divorce deeply painful.

Moving on from our marriage was overwhelming at best. It involved uprooting the lives of our young children, relocation, working out our vehicle situation, and the big D. In addition, we were forced to face a future of acclimating outside of couple hood, eventually meeting and dating new people. I didn't want to *have* to move on, yet I had to move on.

The first time I broached the subject of divorce with my kids was a colossal failure. I didn't know how to handle such a delicate topic, but tried my best. I never imagined having such a conversation with my children.

I was snuggling with my daughter in bed one afternoon, chatting about this and that. I loved my time with her, and tagged her as an old soul not long after her birth. As we cocooned ourselves under the covers I asked, "Do you have any friends with divorced parents?"

"Yes," she replied, and provided me a list of names from among her classmates.

"What do you think it would look like if daddy and I were divorced?"

"I don't think anything would be different," she said confidently. "You never talk to each other except about money." What an observation for such a little girl. At the time of our chat, she was right. Then she said something which took me aback: "I know what true love looks like, mom, and this isn't it."

You're probably asking yourself what a nine-year-old could possibly know about true love, but that's the thing about her wisdom – it's beyond her years.

My son walked into the bedroom and hopped up on the bed to join the snuggle fest. After the exchange with my daughter, I had a little more confidence about the topic and chose to ask him the same question. He provided the perfect opening.

"What are you talking about?" he asked.

I forged ahead.

"We were discussing divorce. If daddy and I were divorced, what do you think that would look like?"

Without only a slight hesitation, he railed with indignation.

"You promised you would never get divorced! You promised God and you promised me!"

Tears filled his cornflower blue eyes. Beside me, tears coated my daughter's rosy cheeks, despite her earlier aloofness. I pulled back and didn't push the issue further. I was a complete failure to my children. If I did not believe it prior to our emotional exchange, I certainly walked away knowing it to be fact.

Our actual separation came months after the scene in my bedroom. The seed I'd planted with our children took root and made the truth of our ending marriage less of a shock. They told me they didn't understand why we would choose to stay unhappily married just for them. I guess we didn't do our part in explaining how much parents sacrifice in doing what they believe is in the best interests of their children. We were no different. If we were not parents, our marriage would've ended much sooner than it did.

Divorce forces a couple to broach topics they never thought they would. Child custody was a non-issue for us, as we believe each parent is important in the lives of their children. Time spent should be equal, or at least fit with the needs of the children. We chose to work together and co-parent without the drama and strife known to plague others. This is our biggest, most significant parenting success so far. Not only are we doing it amicably, we are selflessly putting their needs above our own. Their needs have changed and evolved since our initial split and we've adapted accordingly. It isn't always easy, but they are worth it.

We opted out of Friend of the Court mediation. I grew up with divorced parents and knew what it felt like to be a financial pawn. My dad spent most of my childhood with bartending jobs that paid under the table so he could avoid his child support responsibility. My mom never said a word about it, but I knew our dire financial situation was a direct result of her two deadbeat ex-husbands. I didn't want the same for my children. Luckily, I knew their dad, as a man of integrity, would never abandon his kids. We may not have married the right people, but we divorced the right people. Knowing your ex's core values provides comfort during the difficult period of divorce.

Property and money were subjects that didn't warrant disagreement or battle. His money was his, and mine was mine. I did not lay claim to his retirement savings, the cash in his bank account, or the home in his name. I walked away with my clothes, keepsakes, and a few furniture items for the kids. Mostly, I looked forward to establishing myself brand new.

Aside from that, I didn't want our children to have everything ripped away. They needed familiarity, which was what they had by me leaving as much in place as possible.

Deciding when and where to relocate was one of my most challenging decisions. We lived in a city of high-priced rentals and little vacancy. I found an apartment community nestled within the heart of a desirable residential neighborhood. Best of all, it was within walking distance of the kids' schools and their dad's house. I made the location decision based on what was best for the kids and in support of their relationship with their dad. Sure, I could have found somewhere more affordable in another town, but this was about them, not me. I made the financial concessions necessary to make our transition easier.

At the end of the day, the kids stayed in the same schools, in the same neighborhood, and with two parents who love them. They were each shown respect for their feelings as our family dynamic evolved through divorce. While nobody makes it out unscathed by such an event, I hope our choices as parents and partners caused as little damage as possible. We all end up in the therapy chair discussing our parents at some point, recounting their weaknesses and failures. Maybe, just maybe, our kids will have a few positive commentaries when their time comes.

Miss Independent

Aside from a brief period in my early twenties, I never lived independently of my parents or spouse until I was thirty-seven. When the time came to leave my marital home and build a new life, I felt both terrified and excited. I relished the thought of creating an environment as a unique reflection of me. Since I chose not to take much from the house I shared with my ex-husband, my slate was clean to do just that.

I found a condominium-like rental unit nestled within a neighborhood of single-family homes. It worked for my children, our open-door policy with their dad, and me. Living less than a mile from where we started provided familiarity and a sense of continuity. Our physical residence changed, but our surroundings did not.

I received a tremendous amount of support and encouragement, and offers of muscle on moving day. A housewarming party hosted by a dear friend and colleague provided basic items to populate my kitchen's cupboards and drawers, as well as a chance to show my guests around. One of my best friends gifted me a shopping trip to outfit my bathrooms. It seemed everyone who knew me was cheering me on to a more fulfilling life. They believed in me. I am glad they did, too, because I did not quite believe in myself. I was still very much like a newborn calf with wobbly legs. My mind had not yet caught up, so I trusted my handy autopilot to get me through the transition.

***

Waking up in my own apartment, in my own bed, was nothing short of exhilarating. I snuggled into the warmth of my new bedding, eyes closed, and took a deep, soul-cleansing breath. I'd become familiar with the smell and sounds of my new home sometime during the night. It dawned on me, as I stretched out my legs to the end of the mattress, I was about to define my new morning routine. That first step onto the plush, beige carpet was literally the first step of my new life as Miss Independent.

My morning unfolded in slow motion, it seemed. Maybe it was my attempt at savoring every moment of newness - the texture of my terrycloth robe as it slipped along my skin and the morning sun as it poured in from the oversize window in the living room.

In the kitchen, I added water to my stainless steel kettle and patiently waited for it to boil. I'd switched to instant coffee - it didn't make sense to brew a full pot for one person. Not a terrible concession, in my opinion.

My favorite mug filled with steaming coffee, and dressed with French vanilla creamer, I sat down at the dining room table. I looked out at the forest-like scene that was my new back yard, I knew I was where I belonged.

As birds chirped their morning singsong, I experienced a moment of deep inner peace, a divine knowing, that I would be okay. I took a photo of my coffee mug and house key, and posted it to Facebook with the caption, "Mine."

The first months were fun for the kids and me. They enjoyed living close to their favorite park, and having an indoor swimming pool located in our neighborhood clubhouse. We quickly adapted and forged a team bond. They seemed to adjust well with their visitation times at dad's house. It was a period of learning for all of us, but especially for me. I learned how to create and follow a new budget, pay bills, and shoulder the reality of no safety net should I fail.

Not everything was rosy in my new life, however. My biggest struggle fell during visitation periods. I sat in my recliner, wine glass beside me, and cried. It was a debilitating kind of loneliness. I missed my babies - their laughter, smiles, and cuddles. The energy in our home was flat in their absence. I often wondered if I'd made a mistake.

My divorced friends with children assured me the loneliness would pass. They lovingly advised me to find a hobby, and to get out and meet people. It would be worse if I stayed home and wallowed, they warned.

The first time my girlfriends came over prior to a night out on the town was magical. The days of getting ready to go out had long past, or so I thought. That night, however, I felt like a twenty-something again! We blasted the stereo, did our hair, teased and laughed. I changed my outfit at least four times before settling on the perfect look. The scene was something new to the adult me. I absorbed each moment of pure happiness. Eventually, it was time to start dating, or at least, think about dating. The emotions and trepidation that plagued this part of my independence was understandable given my history. Marriage provided safety from the harm and abuse I felt vulnerable to as a single woman. For me, there existed a dating learning curve. Although I was nervous, I welcomed all new experiences that awaited.

My first "experience" was a professional softball player. We met at a local watering hole during a night out with friends. He was in town with his team playing in an international tournament – the softball version of the World Series. The moment our eyes met bred mutual interest and attraction. He was kind, non-threatening, and just a tad too forward. He possessed a heady mix of confidence, masculinity, and thoughtfulness. He didn't push me in conversation, and took only what I freely offered. We covered a wide range of topics, mostly centered on the differences and similarities between men and women. Our banter eventually tapered off, morphing into intense eye contact and loaded silence.

"Can I kiss you?" he asked.

"No." I quickly replied, my nerves on edge.

"Can I hold your hand?"

"Yes," I whispered, desiring to know what his skin felt like against mine. It had been so long.

He reached for my right hand, brushing his soft, plush lips across my knuckles. He entwined his fingers with mine and rested our connected hands in his lap. We sat together quietly, observing the drunk, obnoxious antics around us. Eventually we drifted back into conversation, where he told me about his softball career and his life in Canada.

We parted ways that evening, but met up again the next day. I won't bore you with the details, but he pulled me out of a slump and provided me the confidence I needed going forward as a single woman with a healthy appetite. He was the antidote to my repression. We had no formal plans to keep in contact, but like all best-laid plans, that flew out the window. We genuinely liked each other, and found ourselves texting and talking multiple times a day. We saw each other once more during our three-month association.

Long distance relationships, even casual ones, require a level of upkeep. It turned out that he wasn't as confident as he first appeared. He was jealous and clingy in response to my newfound independence. In turn, I found it cumbersome to keep things casual and light. It was good we ended things, but I will always be grateful for that first, post-divorce spark. I came alive. People come into our lives for various reasons. Even though his role was short, it was significant.

From there I entered the world of online dating. What a train wreck! After thoughtfully filling out my dating profile, every burly woodsman and gangbanger came calling. Men who seemed perfectly nice and professional blindsided me with unsolicited pictures of their junk. It seemed honest men with honorable intentions were extinct.

I went on many first dates during my early singlehood. I had a stringent checklist of traits I did not want in a date. When I shared the list with my girlfriends during a work lunch, they laughed and told me I was insane. In their defense, I was quite a judgmental person. My ideal mate was almost inhuman. With the expectations imposed upon my potential suitor, it's no wonder I found my first dates lacking.

Eventually, I met a man who was different. He was a professional like me, and we had an immediate attraction (or maybe it was the wine). The night we met, I recognized his intelligence, his depth, and his sense of humor. We continued to spend time together after our first date, and fell into a routine. He was a serial dater, in his own words, and told me not to fall in love with him. I still chuckle at that.

He was in a dark place as a single dad and missed his children who lived across the state. He'd been through a horrendous divorce that involved infidelity on his wife's part. Emotional turmoil caused him to sink into a deep depression and live with a devil-may-care chip on his shoulder. Since I was also going through the early days of post-divorce life, missing my children and trying to find balance, it was easy to take comfort in his life of seclusion and complacency. There were good memories made between us, and a genuine affection on my part, but he was not for me.

Our friendship ended on a Saturday afternoon, sending me into the arms of my tribe. I felt rejected and sad, knowing he was already searching for someone to take my place. While I was not in love with him, I felt deeply for the things he was going through and wanted to save him. I'm sure there's a therapy session in that! Hearing the old "It's not you, it's me" excuse at thirty-seven was humbling and a bit humiliating. It was me, and it was him - there was never an "us."

What I took away from my new experiences and disappointments was that I had a lot of growing to do. I needed to be alone for a while to explore all the things I'd neglected about myself. It wouldn't serve me to dilute the waters of personal growth with the complications of a romantic relationship.

PART V

Girl on the Right Kicks Ass

"We can only be said to be alive in those moments when our hearts are conscious of our treasures."
-THORNTON WILDER

My Person

In my experience, the sure way to thwart a plan is to declare you have one. I know better, but I consistently fail to refrain from making plans. It was not in my plan to meet a man and fall hopelessly, madly in love. In fact, that was the opposite of my plan.

I was finally in a peaceful place living as the free spirit I suppressed during my marriage. I was not interested in playing by someone else's rules, or allowing myself to be put back into a box, lid slammed shut, and my flame extinguished. Single life was my paradise.

My life took an unexpected detour in 2013 on Easter Sunday. The kids and I spent the day celebrating the death and resurrection of Jesus, as well as the arrival of the Easter Bunny. Since we hadn't colored eggs the week prior, I converted our dining room table into Easter Egg Central. They were in creative heaven and embarked on creating a dozen colorful masterpieces.

I took a few moments alone to delete my online dating accounts. I'd made the decision to focus on other aspects of my life, including my career and financial future. I deleted the first account without incident. Upon logging into the other, the search feature beckoned seductively. Just one more time, I thought. After choosing my desired search filters, I browsed the results. I stopped on one face and thought, "He looks sad." I noticed his location was too far from me and modified the search filters. The same sad faced man appeared as the first result. I thought it was odd and modified my search again. There he was. As I stared at the man's face, perplexed with the search function, a chime sounded to alert me of a private message. I clicked on the envelope icon and found a message from the sad faced man. What are the chances of that? Before I could read or respond to his note, an instant message box popped up on the screen.

"Hi. How are you?"

My fingers danced across the keys, "I'm good, how are you?"

"Life served me up a shit sandwich."

If "shit sandwich" wasn't on my Do Not Want list, consider it added! Besides that, I didn't want a sad man for a companion. I was finally in a good place of peace and relaxation. The last thing I wanted was someone to add his baggage to mine. I had more than enough for a small village. Yet, looking at his profile photo, his eyes especially, I allowed myself to keep the dialog going. What I discovered surprised me.

As we chatted, it was clear this man, although rough around the edges, was intelligent and kind. He was open and honest, and was not out to impress me. I know that sounds odd, especially since we connected through an online dating website. My initial response was not one of romantic interest; I believed the man needed an ear to listen, and somebody to provide perspective and support. That was my bread and butter. I was a "save the world" kind of girl. He picked wisely.

It was more. I'm unable tell you how I knew, but he knew it, too. There are moments and events in life with divine purpose. They are part of a much larger plan, and knowing this, you allow the bigger picture to unfold. For whatever reason, we connected that evening, and the evenings that followed. Eventually he asked if we could talk on the phone. I was hesitant, and he called me out.

"You're afraid," he baited, "Once we hear each other's voices, there's no turning back."

I wondered how this man, who was a stranger not less than a week ago, knew me so well. He nailed it, quite honestly. As I mentioned, there was something at play between us, and it scared me. I was not ready for My Person. My resistance softened, and I found myself listening to a voice that sparked a longing in my heart I'd never experienced. Without a doubt, his was the voice of My Person.

After several days, he informed me quite bluntly he was going to marry me. I replied with my special blend of sarcasm, "Oh, are you?"

"I don't think you understand. I am a decisive person. Once I make up my mind, that's it."

I remained silent, listening as he wove a tale of marrying me on a bridge, a stone bridge, including a meaningful description of the bridge's symbolism of our past, present, and future. I followed his words, not quite believing in the visual he'd painted. A second marriage was not in my plan (there's that word again).

The friendship-relationship we were forging seemed to shift. It was as if our souls settled in. It wasn't infatuation or lust, but completeness - like the deepest sigh my lungs could manage. I felt starved for this man, for the way he saw into me, challenged me, and pushed me to be better. A relationship like ours was a new concept and left me without an example to draw from.

We spent our first months together opening our emotional suitcases and unpacking piece by piece. Some items were heavier than others. Through patience and understanding, we removed a few items permanently and lightened the load. For most relationships, the first months are the honeymoon phase. Not for us. We did a belly flop into a mud puddle.

Blending lifestyles and philosophies, child rearing and exes, was a minefield. We experienced hiccups along the way, some more intense than others. Our commitment to each other, and our desire to build a life together, required us to make compromises and concessions. At times, I kicked and screamed, not at all certain I wanted to do the relationship dance again. It takes a tremendous effort, and I wasn't sure I had the stomach for it. The saying, "Be careful what you wish for because you just might get it." ran through my mind on several occasions.

Partnership was a new to me. In my marriage to a man with Asperger's Syndrome, a traditional state of partnership did not exist. This was no fault of my ex-husband's or mine, it was the nature of the beast. Finding myself in a partnership felt unfamiliar and scary. He called me out repeatedly on issues of courtesy and thoughtfulness. I easily applied these concepts to other areas of my life, but had no experience in the context of a romantic relationship. I told him early on that I didn't know how to be a partner and wasn't sure I'd be any good at it. He reassured me it would be fine. It wasn't always fine, but we've managed to navigate through each challenge.

One of the best parts about our relationship is we understand each other and the issues that drive us. For two people who bear scars that often go unseen to others, it is a relief not having to explain every emotion or reaction. This is the result of being violated and abused by those we'd trusted. Overzealousness on issues of safety and self-preservation often dictates our behavior in response to hurt and insecurity. These issues have nearly broken us on occasion, and prompted us to seek outside help.

Therapy isn't a dirty word in our household. When faced with a situation that nearly ended our relationship, we agreed to face our respective demons. Usually, in these circumstances, people seek couple's therapy, but not us. We knew we had to work independently to achieve the best relationship possible - a strategy that has proven effective so far. We've set hard boundaries, improved communication, and identified specific issues, attitudes, and behaviors that pose a threat to our relationship. In fact, my therapist has mentioned on more than one occasion how she's never seen a couple work as hard as we have.

This is a testament to how far I've come in the realm of partnership. In the battle between fight and flight, I was the epitome of flight. In the presence of hurt, my first instinct is to get away from the situation or person that's hurting me. In the beginning of our relationship, it was a physical manifestation. There were more than a few late-night arguments that prompted me to grab my car keys and run out the front door. Over time, I learned to stay and face my fears. I played the "What is the worst that could happen by staying?" game, and eventually conquered my toxic behavior. This is not to say I don't struggle with an emotional flee, because I do. I am a work in progress.

We came together in marriage, our friends and family as witnesses, and pledged to keep working and healing as a team. We each wrote vows that reflected this promise. Our love has blossomed beyond the word, and our commitment to fight for happily ever after is unshakable. There's outside noise, but we are far better equipped than we were in the beginning.

Although we didn't get married on the stone bridge, the bridge's symbolism, first articulated by My Person, is still relevant as we continue our journey from past to future. I am madly in love with, insanely attracted to, and above all, maintain a deep respect for my new husband - My Person.

A shit sandwich and an online dating site forever changed my life.

CHAPTER 20

His Mine Ours

Finding My Person was a blessing and something I never imagined happening. I wasn't looking, wasn't even interested in finding "The One," but it seems we were the centerpiece of someone else's plan. While it was a blessing, our newfound romance did not come without its complications. The timing couldn't have been worse for My Person, who was still processing a major life crisis.

Do you remember the shit sandwich he mentioned during our first conversation? It was far worse and provided us with hurdles to jump from the first. He was honest about his situation, and the after-effects he was wading through. Maybe it was my mindset at the time, but his disclosures did not alarm me or cause me to recoil from a relationship.

I was in a peaceful, well-adjusted, post-divorce period, and coming to terms with the newness of single life. I was changing from the inside, and growing up in a way that was long overdue. I had a career, healthy children, my own home, a friendship with my former spouse, and a tribe who supported and loved me unconditionally. I was in the zone, as they say.

I believed I was untouchable in my new relationship. I believed his problems were his alone, and had no bearing on me. I suppose I counted on it, in all honesty. That was a gross miscalculation on my part, and quite naive.

Of all the lessons I've learned in our relationship, the concept of partnership was the biggest. Having no real experience in the partnership mosh pit, I flubbed my way through. It was a painful period of intense growth. When you are in a loving relationship, it's nearly impossible to ignore your partner as they drown in emotional pain. My Person was attempting to claw his way out of his darkest days, and I was his life preserver.

The blending of our lives came about much faster than either of us anticipated. After only two months together he moved into the home I shared with my children. I'm sure a few eyebrows rose at that decision, but it was mine to make. My Person needed to relocate and we welcomed him into our home.

I'm shocked we made it through our first six months together without a body bag! To be fair, it goes both ways. I muttered the words, "who does he think he is?" nearly a million times during the first weeks. He did nearly everything the opposite of me, which tipped my world off its axis. We got in each other's way, he touched my stuff, and his baggage oozed all over my peaceful life.

We each struggled with cohabitation and the mingling of children. I've heard horror stories about the unsuccessful blending of families, and prayed hard ours wouldn't end up a statistic. That concern came in second to what his baggage was doing – bringing out my baggage. We had more luggage combined than what a yearlong trip around the world would require.

This is where the concept of "his, mine, and ours" obliterated. Despite what each of us brought to our relationship, it was now a team effort to make our demons dance together politely. There was no room for my rebellious attitude, or his reactive outbursts. We'd both been through hell and had the scars to prove it. Together we learned how to talk about the circumstances that led to each scar, what we've done or need to do to heal, and how to accept each other through the process. Learning each other's origins proved an effective tool during the challenging days of our relationship.

We both have enormous trust issues. His trust issues are relationship-centered, where mine are about safety and survival. These demons, despite our best efforts, do not play well with each other. They feed on our insecurities and pop up uninvited at times of closeness, and as new bonds are forming. Our mental arms flail, emergency alarms sounding loudly in our ears. There doesn't need to be an actual trespass, only what our respective minds create or perceive. We continue to work on this, which is most definitely an "ours."

We've settled in to our life together and found a workable way to blend two lives and families. We identified areas that proved troublesome to our relationship, which was half the battle. We've explored solutions and made necessary concessions to achieve the harmony and balance we each desire.

Nobody is perfect, and everybody deserves acceptance. I could've walked away from a situation that was far from my ideal. That would've also required me to walk away from the person who is my ideal. It's the first time in my life I fought for something despite not knowing whether it would end in success or failure. I fought blindly and fiercely for love.

I am ashamed to admit I let so much of my life pass by without loving and accepting wholly and without prejudice. Like most survivors of trauma, I thought I was safer as an island. In truth, I am far safer with my partner, lover, and friend fighting with me, and for me.

Weightless

After living nearly two decades as a morbidly obese woman, I'd had enough. I carried over 200 lbs. of physical and emotional weight on my 5'3" frame, and it was exhausting. The extra weight wreaked havoc with my health. I knew if I didn't lose weight and deal with my addiction to food, including the underlying issues driving that addiction, I was going to die.

I'm not sure I realized how large I was at 237 lbs. Maybe it was denial, or maybe I was confident in the way I dressed and presented myself. I took care to wear stylish, yet weight appropriate clothes. I indulged in makeup, accessories, and shoes. My efforts provided a mask to cover the real nature of my obesity.

Obesity was a culmination of emotional and mental turmoil that drove me to seek solace in food. I created my obesity to provide a physical barrier from the world. The world was a place of pain, and I was determined to seclude myself, especially physically, from that pain.

I flirted with the idea of weight loss surgery for years. It was more like a fantasy, in truth. I did research on cost and location, and made mental note of surgery requirements. This information resided in the recesses of my mind since I didn't have the financial means to pay for elective surgery. Besides that, my employer and medical insurance carrier excluded this type of procedure. Surgery wasn't a viable option, so I set out to work on my addiction, hoping the rest would fall into place.

I sought help from a therapist who specializes in addiction. She is also well versed in bipolar, which made it a win-win for me. Not long after our intake session I learned of a coming change in my employer's medical insurance policy - the inclusion of weight loss surgery.

Like any decision, I discussed it with my family and friends. Their response was a collective, "You're not that big!" or "You won't qualify, you're not big enough." While I appreciated their need to reassure me I was more than a number on the scale, their years of reassurances fed my denial. At first I threw numbers at them, making a case that I was indeed "big enough" to qualify for bariatric surgery. Sometimes the people who love you most are also the people who enable you to continue down a deadly path. I was done with that, and made the decision to go forward.

I spent a mandatory six months of doctor appointments, weight tracking, and therapy. I met a highly recommended surgeon who described the procedure in detail and answered my questions. I attended nutrition classes where I learned about my pre-surgery diet, and the subsequent food phases during post-surgical months. There were many details to keep track of. Each detail provided me hope for a healthy future.

During a session with a program psychiatrist, I voiced, for the first time, that I was not embarking on surgery for vanity purposes. It never occurred to me I would have more clothing options or look prettier.

My goal was to face the issues that put the weight in place, to retrain my thought patterns and eliminate negative self-talk. I was all about healing from the inside, and hoping, with a ton of hard work, the outside would reflect my new emotional and mental health.

It was about changing my life, self-care, and letting go. I'd lived a life where disappoint was soothed by a Hershey bar, every piece of taffy a cure for despair. I was done with self-destruction.

To facilitate my journey, I joined an online support site for bariatric surgery patients. It was a comprehensive site with thousands of chat threads covering pre- and post-surgery topics. It was overwhelming at best. I joined one of the chats, which led to a breakout group of women from all over the United States.

We started a private Facebook group, and shared our stories, surgery dates, and biggest fears. We bonded quickly. We called ourselves Sleeve Sisters, and provided each other with encouragement and love. Our group eventually dwindled down to five, then four. We are still close, although our focus has moved on from weight issues to life in general.

On April 27, 2015, a surgeon removed over fifty percent of my stomach, leaving a banana-sized pouch. My banana, they told me, would be a valuable tool to help me change my life. It was up to me to make behavior modifications and follow the rules. I wasn't worried about failing. I was dedicated and did an amazing job prior to surgery in eliminating soda and sugar from my diet. I even lost weight before the day I checked into the hospital. I was a success story in the making.

The first six months after surgery were wonderful. I watched the numbers on the scale, as well as my pants size, dwindle with each passing week. I maintained a healthy focus on my progress, and continued modifying my eating and drinking behavior. I'd sworn off alcohol and was dedicated to eating nutrient-rich foods.

I proved many naysayers wrong as they praised my weight loss. Of course, there were those who said I took the easy way out of obesity. I was immune to their ignorance. I spent a great deal of time educating my circle on the benefits of surgery. I explained why I needed immediate results to reverse serious health issues. My only side effect, the one I never expected, was the on my Fibromyalgia symptoms.

I was diagnosed with Fibromyalgia in the fall of 2000. Symptoms began shortly after the birth of my first child, and led me on a medical whodunit for over a year. I was tested for Multiple Sclerosis, Lupus, and Rheumatoid Arthritis prior to my official diagnosis of Fibromyalgia. The neurologist explained my disease would not get better or worse. I would have good days and bad days. This proved true until my weight loss surgery.

Surgery not only exacerbated my symptoms, it provided the catalyst for new symptoms of greater severity. After nearly fifteen years successfully managing symptoms without medication or intervention, my luck ran out. I struggled to get out of bed for months, and fatigued easily with minor provocation. My body experienced debilitating pain. My brain was unfocused and foggy. My doctor prescribed medication to help with my symptoms, and informed me I would have to accept my new normal. He educated me on the importance of getting enough sleep, eliminating unnecessary stress, and listening to my body. I was devastated.

The result of my Fibro complications was hard on my body, and equally hard on my weight loss goal. Since I reserve most of my energy for battling daily pain and fatigue, I have little motivation for anything more than my workday and the occasional activity.

Like every battle that came before, I am determined to push myself beyond my comfort zone and challenge my body. What I love about goals is that you can modify them as much as you need. Forward progress, regardless of pace, is still forward progress.

I traded life threatening health problems for one I can maneuver with thought and care. I remain happy with my surgery choice, celebrate the things I've learned, and how I've grown. A weightlessness has settled within me, and it has nothing to do with my physical body.

Art of Gratitude

I am thankful for the ability to dwell in a place that allows me to appreciate my circumstances, good and bad, and discover purpose beyond the obvious. This is the art of gratitude. Prone to depression and anxiety, it's important for me to stay positive. The practice of gratitude is easiest during times of ease and bounty, but it is most important to practice gratitude in times of struggle and hardship.

After many twists and turns in my career, I found a home working in marketing and public relations with a global technology company. My position allowed me to further develop my skill set, and build critical industry relationships. I found a passion and fire for my work, which provided an outlet to feed both my creative and analytical sides. While not every aspect of my time with the company was perfect, there were numerous opportunities afforded me. I felt on top of the world.

In November 2015, I sat across from my boss and a representative from human resources as they informed me my time with the company was at an end. It was a blow to my gut. I'd worked to brand and market the original company and its spinoff for five years. Despite my desire to yell and rail, I took the high road and didn't create a scene. With grace and dignity, I quietly packed up my desk and carried my box of belongings out the front door. As I exited the parking lot, I watched everything I'd worked for disappear in my rearview mirror.

I wasn't worried about my next step. In some ways, I was relieved to leave my dysfunctional employer behind. Besides, every ending paved the way for a new beginning. With a head full of optimism, I drove to the unemployment office and applied for benefits to get me through.

It never occurred to me I would be unemployed for nearly six months. I woke every morning to a routine of coffee and job hunting. I utilized every contact in my network for leads. It was too close to the holidays, they told me, and nobody was hiring. I submitted hundreds of online applications and resumes, and sat through more than a dozen interviews. The results were always the same: I was overqualified.

Some interviews were memorable. One interviewer told me to "dumb it down" in future interviews. Being me, I told him maybe he should bring it up a bit. Who in the hell did he think he was, anyway? I'd worked hard to gain the experience and knowledge that propelled me in my career.

Knowing my stubborn streak, I sought counsel from a trusted mentor and friend. Having worked with me as an agency partner through the years, he provided valuable perspective. While I didn't need to dumb it down, in his opinion, I did need to think about perception. If an interviewer perceived that I could do their job, or felt threatened that I could do it better, I wouldn't get the job I was interviewing for. He told me to contain my awesomeness. We had a good laugh over that, but there was also a grain of truth in his message. Going forward, I needed a new interview strategy.

Six months of unemployment took its toll, as you can imagine. Like most people, I didn't have a deep enough emergency fund in place. I was a single mom of two teenagers who struggled to provide necessities. I found myself at the mercy of dear friends for donations of groceries and gas money, among other things. Worse, I was facing the inevitable circumstance of losing my rental house. It was a stressful period of uncertainty and despair. I didn't know where to turn or how to dig myself out of the rubble.

During this time, a few members of my tribe were writing daily Facebook posts of gratitude. I read along, knowing each of my friends and their situations. I commented faithfully, yet never made a post of my own. Instead, I felt inspired to create a Facebook group and write uplifting posts full of positivity and gratitude. I went public with my situation, exposing my fears and struggles. In the core of my pain, I found gratitude and hope. I changed my surroundings, along with the energy I allowed in my environment. I banished negativity from my mind and renewed my spirit. It was an incredible transformation!

The time I spent in a gratuitous state allowed me to persevere. I even purchased a stone with the word "Gratitude" etched on one side. My gratitude stone went everywhere with me, and sometimes rested in the warmth of my palm on the most difficult days. Some would call my stone a relic of superstition; I found comfort in the word, and in the art of practice.

A rather prolific episode of bipolar depression reared its ugly head. I was compromised mentally and emotionally from worry, which provided an in. This is when I lost my house officially, and panicked at the thought of being separated from my children. I knew their dad would take them in, but I was facing the reality of finding a shelter for myself. I reached out to friends in the nonprofit sector to feel out my options. There were no shelters in my area.

With a broken heart, I approached my ex-husband about taking in our kids. He readily agreed, as I knew he would. Because of the friendship we'd maintained since our divorce, he offered me a home as well. It wasn't ideal, but it was a relief to know I would stay with my children. The kids moved in to their childhood bedrooms, and I set up a living space in the finished basement.

I don't think anyone, including me, believed I would be out of work for so long. I also couldn't have predicted how being "overqualified" would prevent me from being hirable. After many years giving my time, my family's time, and neglecting friendships and hobbies during my career, I lost sight of who I was without the backdrop of an office and work family. It was that void, grief for what I'd lost, which caused me to sink deep into depression. I cried more tears than I knew I had. I was out of fight. I felt like a failure as a mother, partner, woman, and human being. I went from hero to zero in the blink of an eye.

Knowing I had to change my job-hunting strategy, I debated looking outside of my home state. Friends from Tennessee and Texas reached out with job prospects and news of booming economies. Desperation caused me to consider the impossible. The very thought of leaving everything and everyone behind rendered me immovable. That's where I was – facing the impossible.

I voiced the idea to my family and faced mixed reviews. What I felt forced to do battled what I wanted to do. I wanted to stay with my children, but forced to find employment. Decision made, I browsed out-of-state job postings. That night, in the darkness and solitude of my basement bedroom, I prayed for God to take me in my sleep. I didn't just pray, I begged.

God didn't take me that night, much to my dismay. I woke up as usual and went about my morning routine. Nothing had changed, but it was about to.

The phone rang as I sipped my second mug of coffee. Deliverance from the past six months came in the form of a job offer from a well-established company only three miles from my basement home. Although it wasn't as lucrative or as highly visible as my previous role, it came with medical insurance and a retirement package, among other benefits. It was an opportunity to start over and regain my confidence. That job offer likely saved my life.

I learned a lot about myself during my unemployment period. Mostly, I learned humility. For years, I'd bought into the idea I would always come out on top. While not a bad outlook to have, I discovered I lacked the stamina to hang in there and have faith. Like so many others, I was spoiled in a world of instant gratification. When I wasn't hired within my first week of joblessness, I mentally gave up. Hindsight is a blessing and a curse.

I also learned that I could live without many things. These days I choose thrifting at Goodwill over paying astounding markups at big box retailers. I now find joy in thirty-five cent used paperbacks over slick new hardcovers. I turn lights off when leaving a room, and never let water run while brushing my teeth. I am grateful for these lessons. It was a time of growth, albeit painfully.

Girl on the Right Defined

I am The Girl on the Right. I am no longer ashamed of my choices and actions, or of those forced upon me. I've spent most of my existence in a befuddled state, living a life upside down. I worked to process each trauma, learning experience, and harsh critique the best I could. I believed the ugliness that touched my life made me unlovable and unworthy. I felt like a target, and often railed at God: "Why me? What have I done to deserve this?"

I am not that girl anymore. I have gained confidence and wisdom, discernment and compassion. While I remain uncertain why my abusers chose me, I have stopped asking why. What matters most is what I do with life's lessons, even those learned in pain. With each new experience and step forward, I forced myself to face my fears, anxieties, and hesitations, and fix the fixable.

I will never be perfect. I've accepted that certain fact as well. Despite years of therapy, medication, and changes in routine and environment, life remains challenging at times. I'm no longer afraid of uncertainty (for the most part). I feel content with my scars. I've downsized my baggage collection to a single carryon. I no longer live in the past. It took me awhile to move forward. Regret is a shady bitch. It makes you long for things that weren't meant for you. For years, I pined for a lost relationship, believing if I'd chosen differently the landscape of my life would be happier, less stressful, and more adventurous.

I've wasted too much time wading through regret.

I choose to look forward. I see things for what they are. Looking forward is acknowledging and accepting truth. I made choices, for my own reasons, and have learned and grown through good and bad consequences. I own it.

Everyone deserves a second chance. I didn't always subscribe to this way of thinking, and have most likely missed out on friendships, relationships, and opportunities because of it. My survival instinct told me to run from hurt. A simple misunderstanding with someone I love caused us to lose ten years of friendship. A lack of forgiveness is more damaging than forgiving could ever be.

Through my journey, I have burned bridges. We all burn a bridge or two before the end of our story. I've learned that forgiveness is not always about me. Sometimes it's for the people who have hurt me. Sometimes it is for others who witness our example.

I am a free spirit. I believed my non-conformist, free-spirited nature was a character flaw. I spent years of self-loathing this part of me. My brain's ability to shift gears quickly is a result of needing to be agile and flexible to survive.

My brain changes directions faster than most people blink. Aside from my survival instinct, this is a product of bipolar disorder. You can imagine how surprised I was to learn my friends love the impulsive part of me. My more structured, uptight friends often find themselves living vicariously through animated tales of unexpected twists and turns. Being impulsive prevents me from being bored - and boring.

I have no desire to fit in with society's unattainable standards. I have fashion faux pas, and leave the house without makeup on. I say "fuck" a lot, among other words. I love sparkly things and have a killer shoe collection. I hate getting dirty. Sometimes I am too loud and boisterous, other times I am quiet and observant. I am a beautiful contradiction.

I've learned to appreciate that I do not fit everywhere, or with everyone. Being unique is far better than being basic. Unique is memorable.

I used to go into an emotional fetal position if something went wrong. I couldn't see past the struggle to get to a solution. I whined about my poor luck and how bad things always happened to me. I was a victim of my own making. Negative self-talk prevented me from seeing and utilizing resources to better my situation.

I am capable. I recognize my power and put it to use. When faced with struggle, I gather my resources and make shit happen.

I am no longer silent. I emerged from a self-imposed box. I constructed an early adult life out of fear and the need for safety. I didn't stand up for myself or causes I believe in. Now I am fierce. I despise injustice, and have no qualms stepping in or stepping up. I feel passionately about social and human rights issues. I will never allow anyone, including me, to get in the way of doing what is right. I will break down doors slammed in my face.

I thought I was dumb. I was creative and whimsical, unfocused and impulsive. I had difficulty "buckling down," as my mom always said. I had trouble with math and mechanical concepts. I struggled in classrooms with strict rules and monotone professors.

I am smart. My intelligence lies in the way I strategize and plot. I create worlds from words. I have people skills and a head for business. I will never be a master of trigonometry or physics, and I am fine with that. I have my own brand of brilliance.

Most of my life, I lacked self-worth. I did not feel a sense of belonging with my family, classmates, co-workers, or friends. The voice inside my head told me I was odd and awkward. I was the loneliest person at the party, the girl who stood outside of the group, never insinuating herself for fear of rejection. I knew the pain of rejection well, remembering the early years when my own parent deserted me.

Now I am confident. I laugh robustly and dance like no one is watching. I sing in the car as if I'm performing at Madison Square Garden. I walk with my head up, eyes forward, and a smile on my face. I belong. The voice still whispers from time to time, "You're not good enough."

"Shut up, bitch." I smugly reply.

I don't have time for negative self-talk, I am too busy kicking ass.

I used to be selfish. My sole focus rested on my survival and getting what I needed. I was not charitable, compassionate, or emotionally connected to others. I didn't accept others' mistakes, despite my own.

I have learned to give, and feel much more at peace with my soul. I do not give begrudgingly, but from a place of human compassion. I accept my own errors, and learn from each trespass. I encourage others to do the same. I volunteer my time, talent, and treasure to give back. I've developed empathy for those who are stuck along their journey. I mentor, counsel, and inspire. When people leave my company, I make them feel valued.

I did not believe I was lovable. I forged a life of conditional love in response to that feeling. In turn, I did not commit to loving anyone fully for fear of rejection.

I am loved. I see love around me in the actions of my friends, children, and spouse. They continue to love me, even when I am difficult to love. They support me in times of need. I have been the recipient of great acts of charity and kindness during challenging times. When I voice a need, people who love me come to my aid. I receive words of encouragement and support daily. Those who love me are my champions and never doubt my ability to achieve my goals with gusto.

My children are forgiving and patient with their imperfect parent. My husband withstands the worst of my baggage, but loves me through the healing process. He stays by my side, is my voice when I need him to be, and makes sure I know I am loved without condition.

While I still face challenges in life, I am far more equipped to take each one on with grace. There is no freer feeling than owning your past, healing in the present, and working toward the future. I have done this, nobody did it for me. Doing so has proved a strength I did not know existed. I am a badass survivor. Looking around me, I see that I have surpassed surviving. I believed surviving others, and myself, was the finish line. There is no finish line in surviving. You must surpass survival to thrive. It is possible to build a life of beauty and possibility, of success and wisdom. It is in you, and it was in me all this time.

Freedom is in thriving. *I am the Girl on the Right.*

Caterpillar to Butterfly

-MARY ELISABETH KENT

My larva is cracking

The life cycle of the butterfly has begun,

Little tiny caterpillar

Stringing webs of silk,

Simple eyes looking,

Spinnerets spinning,

Prolegs working,

Growing, growing faster.

Chrysalis at last.

Days and days go by.

Finally emerging, slowly as I go

Now I'm a big beautiful butterfly,

Fluttering as I fly free.

Made in the USA
Middletown, DE
12 September 2019